D1590031

Other books in the Vietnam series by Bill Norris

Flying Into The Storm

# Dagger Four Is OK
## Brig. Gen. Norman C. Gaddis
## P. O. W. Memoir

By
Bill Norris

ISBN 978-0-9915409-3-8
Library of Congress Control Number: 2015906377

Published by Nekko Books LLC
www.nekkobooks.com
Email: info@nekkobooks.com

Edited by C. E. Wertheimer

Cover art by:
Sheila Norris
Nekko Books LLC

Cover:
Original photo taken by the North Vietnamese immediately upon the
capture of Colonel Norman C. Gaddis, F-4 Pilot, on May 12, 1967.
General Gaddis was asked by the U.S. Government in the early 1990's to
review a batch of photographs retrieved from the North Vietnamese to
see if he recognized anyone. He was amazed to discover his own photo.
He knew it was taken immediately since they stripped him of his flight
suit as soon as he was taken prisoner.

# Acknowledgements

*To Charley Wertheimer, Editor. Your friendship, patience and determination were invaluable in the completion of this most worthwhile and historical project.*

*To Sheila Norris, my wife and life partner. Your loving belief and support keep the words flowing.*

# *POW Lament*

Sitting alone in this dark place, have no one here to share my space,
Have no pillow for my head, just one thin blanket for my bed;
Nobody here to keep me sane, there's no one else to feel my pain.
How can it be so cold when it's just a summer rain?

It's been so long since I felt love, no smile or sign from the Lord above;
I'm in need of a human touch, never knew that it could mean so much.
Just need someone to give me a hand, need a shave but don't think I can;
My body aches, my back is bent, yet I know a doctor won't be sent.

To get to this place I felt such a fool, how can my world be so cruel?
Now as I sit here in the cold, I can feel my body growing old;
I can only see the gloom, as I stare at the four walls of this room.
A thousand days and long lonely nights, I need a friend to share my plight.

When I feel I can't go on, there's a glimmer of light in the crack of dawn,
For in my dreams I can see my past, and know this current hell won't last.
I reach for you, arms open wide, I'll be a man and keep my pride;
I lean on my faith to carry me through, and I hope it will bring me back to you.

But for now, how can it be so cold, when it's just a summer rain?

*-Bill Norris*

# Dedication

For her devotion, her undying love, her strength, her wisdom, her unshakable faith in Him and me, for her days and months of agony, for her steadfastness in shaping the lives and values of our two sons, for constantly rejecting the idea that there can be no tomorrow, I dedicate this work to my wife, Hazel Lee.

Norman C. Gaddis

# Preface

This is my personal account of my military career and my experiences as a prisoner of war in North Vietnam for almost six years. The facts are true and no effort has been made to embellish them. I have long wanted to document my experiences while I was confined in the infamous North Vietnamese Hoa Lo Prison, facetiously named "The Hanoi Hilton" by my colleagues, some of whom arrived there almost three years before me.

I was successful returning to society and even in resuming my military career after my release. When I retired from the Air Force, Hazel and I purchased a lot next to the thirteenth green in Bermuda Run, a gated community near Winston-Salem, North Carolina. On that lot we built the home I had carefully constructed in my mind while enduring one thousand days as a POW in solitary confinement. Designing and building that home in my dream world helped to maintain my sanity.

After my retirement, my private goal of writing the story of my capture and captivity kept eating at me. While I was able to write down experiences, I was finding it hard to bring it together in a readable manuscript. In the midst of my struggling, I was fortunate to be able to renew my friendship with Bill Norris.

Hazel and I met Bill and his wife, Sheila, back in the early 1990's when they moved into Bermuda Run. Bill was also a Vietnam veteran and Hazel and I became immediate friends with them. They subsequently moved to Florida, but we stayed in touch.

In March of 2014, Bill published his book, *Flying Into The Storm*, which documents his experiences as an infantryman. Having shared many of our stories with each other when we were both in Bermuda Run, he sent me an autographed copy. I was mesmerized by his straight forward writing style that took me with him through his year in combat. My own memories flashed through my mind as I was reading and my desire to share my experiences with others was reinvigorated.

I wrote Bill a letter complimenting him on his book and sharing with him how energized I was by reading it. After receiving my letter, Bill called and asked if I would like to have him tell my story for me. He said it was a story that needed to be told.

I gratefully accepted Bill's offer because I had been incentivized by two significant events to share my experiences. The first was the completion and dedication of the Vietnam Veterans Memorial in Washington. It seemed to signify to veterans like me of that unpopular war that America was, in a strange sort of way, trying to say "Thank you for your sacrifices." Rarely has any monument to America's veterans evoked such emotions as we watched relatives and friends search the long, black, V-shaped marble monument to find the name of a loved one who died half a world away.

The second event was the final interment of the remains of a Vietnam veteran in the Tomb of the Unknowns at Arlington National Cemetery. One could not witness that solemn ceremony without feeling compassion for the family who would never know that their loved one was honored on that day and for the families of the twenty-four hundred Americans still missing in Southeast Asia. I harbored the knowledge that my family could easily have been a member of that terrible club. I know first-hand from the accounts from my family that the months and years spent not knowing is the most grueling and punishing experience one can endure short of being themselves missing or in captivity.

The passage of time is a desperately welcomed healer that has the ability to take our most difficult memories and lock them away in our minds' secret vault, allowing those of us who served the opportunity to move forward and live our lives as normally as possible. However, the harsh realities of war and the price we pay both individually and as a nation must be remembered and acknowledged for all time by those who are empowered to decide the fate of our men and women who dedicate themselves to the service of their country.

Hopefully, this work will help others to remember and reflect on the consequences of sending our sons and daughters off to war.

I was born to fly.

I should have been delivered into this

world with wings attached.

I guess God must have wanted me to

earn them.

# Chapter 1

The latter part of 1964 saw American involvement in Vietnam intensify. The North Vietnam insurgents sent troops and equipment into Cambodia and Laos and began to establish regular troop and supply movements up and down what would become known as the Ho Chi Minh Trail that wove in and out of Vietnam, Laos and Cambodia. The South Vietnamese were incapable of holding off the insurgents from North Vietnam who were attacking targets near Saigon.

President Johnson authorized American ground forces to engage the insurgents. Boots on the ground, the United States was now immersed in the conflict. American pilots who had been flying rear seat as advisors to the ARVN (Army Regular Vietnam) pilots were now flying the attack airplanes with South Vietnamese pilots sitting in the back seat. It was a necessary role reversal if air superiority was to be maintained.

In February of 1965, the U.S. began to bomb targets in the southern part of North Vietnam. To implement the change in strategy, America began a massive buildup of U.S. Army and Air Force units in support of its rapidly escalating involvement.

At that point in time, I was completing a tour of duty in the Pentagon which would end in July. While I had not given much thought as to where I would be assigned next, it was rumored that I was being considered for a staff assignment at NATO in Oslo, Norway. Coincidentally, in July, before I had received new assignment orders, the Air Force announced its list for the Senior Service Schools. I was selected to attend the National War College at Fort McNair in Washington, DC. It came as a complete surprise to me since I was a very junior Lieutenant Colonel. The National War College was for mid-level managers and senior military officers and I had not held a command position, such as a Wing Commander or Base Commander. I was pleasantly surprised. The real up side was that our family could remain in Falls Church.

The class consisted of one hundred thirty-six men from the Armed Forces and at least one person from each of the major government agencies. It was a diverse group of people with an assigned curriculum in the field of International Relations.

There were no foreign students in the class although our primary speakers were from International Military Organizations such as NATO and SEATO, diplomats from the U.S. State Department and world trade organizations. We, the students, were required to write a thesis on a subject related to our studies. I chose to write on the subject of "Australia and Its Strategic Importance to the Unites States." Circumstances in Vietnam prompted our program directors to add Southeast Asia to all of our assignments.

A feature of the class was to break out at midpoint and travel to countries involved in our thesis along with other students whose subject focused on the same region. Our Australia-Southeast Asia focus group consisted of forty students and instructors.

In December, before our Pacific trip would commence, Mother called to tell me that Dad was in the hospital with severe kidney failure and he was not expected to survive. Two days after Christmas he had slipped into a coma. I notified the college of his condition and was allowed to take an emergency leave. Hazel and I arrived in Knoxville just before he passed away on December 29, 1965. Dad was only sixty-three years old.

When we returned home to Falls Church on January 4, 1966, I departed on the War College trip to the Pacific Area that would last almost three weeks. Our focus group traveled to Hawaii first to attend a general military briefing on the state of the entire Pacific area. The primary focus of concern was the ongoing conflict in South Vietnam.

After Hawaii, our trip included conferences in Australia, Malaysia and Thailand. Lastly, we attended a special briefing and assessment of the Vietnam situation during our final stop in the Philippines. There were few words of encouragement regarding the military outlook or hope for any kind of favorable early resolution to the conflict.

Upon completion of our travels and as graduation approached, I had high hopes that I would get the rumored NATO assignment in Norway. However, when the orders list was released, I was assigned to the 12th Tactical Fighter Wing at Cam Ranh Bay, South Vietnam. I later learned that Colonel Jones E. Bolt, the commander of the 12th Wing who I was stationed with at Neubiberg, Germany from 1950 to 1952, had requested me. He was a seasoned Wing commander having commanded a fighter wing in Okinawa for three years.

The news of an overseas combat assignment at this point in my career was not what I hoped for either for me or my family. When war broke out after the bombing of Pearl Harbor, I had gladly volunteered for service. I fully expected to fly prolonged fighter missions in that war and was disappointed that my training took too long for me to be included, especially after the death of my brother who was killed during the invasion of Omaha Beach in 1944.

I knew that the purpose of my years of training as a fighter pilot was to prepare me to represent my country in war. I truly never expected that my military path would lead me to Southeast Asia to get involved in a war in an obscure country that had a history of prolonged and unresolved conflict.

The hardest call I ever made to my wife, Hazel, was to inform her of my news about Vietnam. It was more than the fact that I would be going off to war. More importantly, we would be separated for an extended period at a stage when I felt that our family needed me the most. The death of my father weighed heavily on me and I knew my mother would fret terribly for a second son to be going into harms' way.

Once the initial shock of the news began to ease, it was time for us to plan for Hazel's and our son Tony's life without me for the coming year. With Steve, our other son, now in college at Duke University, there was no compelling reason for her to remain in the Washington area. It would be more practical for her to be near family. Therefore, we decided Hazel and Tony should consider moving to Winston-Salem to be near her Mom during my absence.

Before we could get comfortable with a decision, we learned that Hazel's mother, Lola, had been diagnosed with ovarian cancer. At the same time, I learned that I would need to go to MacDill Air Force Base in Tampa for eighteen weeks of training to fly the F-4C airplanes since I had not qualified in them.

We drove to Winston-Salem to visit with Lola and to meet with her doctors. Their unfortunate diagnosis was that she could be expected to live for two or three more years at most. There was no longer a question where Hazel needed to go during my absence. At the same time, learning that Lola's circumstance did not require Hazel to be with her right now, it allowed Hazel to accompany me to Tampa for the first few months of my training. We immediately requested that the Air Force place our furniture in temporary storage for ninety days.

I started thinking about Hazel's needs while I would be away. Our car was six years old so we decided to purchase a new Pontiac Tempest. I would feel much better knowing she was driving a reliable car.

Starting in the latter part of May, I was scheduled to be in flight training at MacDill for about four and a half months, so we rented temporary housing in an apartment at Madeira Beach near St. Petersburg. I cherished every hour I was able to spend with my family knowing that when this training assignment ended, I would be leaving them for a year.

Tony had to be registered for school by late August so we invited Steve to come from Durham to spend two weeks with us before Hazel had to leave for Winston-Salem and Steve had to be back to start the fall semester at Duke. We rented a small trailer for our belongings, and Steve helped me with the drive to Winston-Salem. Hazel's step-father rented us a three-bedroom apartment near Tony's school. As soon as they were settled in I returned to MacDill to finish my training and moved into the Visiting Officers Quarters. The training moved along smoothly. By October 1, 1966, I had flown over seventy-five hours in the F-4C.

Shortly thereafter, the Air Force promotion list came out and I was promoted to Colonel effective on October 20. I was both stunned and humbled. In eighteen years, I had risen from a lieutenant to the rank of Colonel. The average time for that accomplishment was twenty-one years. Hazel was elated and proud for me when I called to tell her the news. I was happy that my new rank would provide higher pay for me to send her and improved benefits for her in my absence. The sad part was that Hazel was not there to pin on my new rank.

I flew to Winston-Salem to enjoy my final two weeks of leave with family before heading out of country. As expected, nobody was thrilled about my assignment to Vietnam. The days seemed to fade one into the next and before it seemed possible, it was time for my departure.

On November 2, Hazel drove me to the Triad Regional Airport between Winston-Salem and Greensboro, and after emotional farewells, I boarded my commercial flight to San Francisco. The flight of four and a half hours gave me a lot of time to reminisce about my past and to ponder my immediate future.

# Chapter 2

Like anyone going off to war for the first time, I was on an emotional roller coaster. I hated leaving Hazel behind once again to deal with all of the family issues. As always, she had steeled herself to showing only positive emotions to Tony and to reassure me that she knew I would be returning safely to her once this assignment ended. She was her usual experienced take-charge military bride and I loved her dearly.

In the midst of all the sentimental emotion, I was also experiencing a fascinating adrenalin rush that was a combination of excitement to be doing what I had trained for years to do together with a stomach wrenching fear of the unknown. I knew only that I was going to join the 12th Tactical Fighter Wing and to fly F-4C jets based on my training at MacDill, but I had no idea what my job would entail. I had a typical itch as a fighter pilot to get into combat but also a secret hope to be assigned to an operations support and/or training position. My day dreaming was interrupted when our flight landed in San Francisco.

I boarded a bus in San Francisco that took me to Travis Air Force Base. The next morning, November 3, I departed by military transport to Hawaii. After a refueling stop, we continued on to the Philippines.

Upon my arrival in the Philippines, I was sent to an escape and survival training school. On the third day of school, I was directed to withdraw from the school and proceed to Cam Ranh Bay. The Deputy for Operations was ready to rotate back to the States and he wanted to go to Hong Kong for five days of rest and relaxation. They needed me to fill in during his absence until the new Deputy arrived. I was not a happy camper to have to cut my survival training short. I hoped that I would not regret missing the survival techniques covered in those sessions.

The wing was flying missions day and night and I would be responsible for all of the flight operations. I did have an experienced assistant to share the responsibility with me. The new Deputy of Operations, Colonel Travis McNeil, was not scheduled to arrive on base for another ten days. He and I were classmates at the National War College and we also knew one another in Germany in 1949.

Colonel Jones Bolt welcomed me on base and helped me with the operational planning pending Colonel McNeil's arrival. Since Cam Ranh Bay was a main staging base for military airlift flights in and out of South Vietnam, we had medical evacuation flights arriving and departing at all hours of the day and night. We also had civilian contract airline flights operating from the base twenty-four hours a day shuttling new replacement troops

9

into country and taking others who were finishing their tours back to the world.

When Travis McNeil arrived, we agreed that he would supervise all daytime flying and I would supervise all night time operations. Colonel Bolt and his deputy, Colonel Thorvaldson, had a similar agreement. I was surprised to learn that the four of us senior officers would fly combat missions regularly with the squadron pilots. I had gotten my wish to be given responsibility for operations but now I knew that my job would include flying regular daily combat missions.

During the ensuing months, we flew most of our missions in South Vietnam to support infantry brigades, to attack targets based on intelligence reports about enemy activity and to disrupt North Vietnamese operations on the Ho Chi Minh Trail. Occasionally, our wing was tasked to fly missions to North Vietnam.

I went to Ubon, Thailand and flew some missions along the borders of Laos and Cambodia with their pilots and then returned to Cam Ranh Bay. A week later, I was sent to Da Nang Air Base to fly missions with that F-4 wing. While I was there, I was scheduled to fly a mission against a target in the southwest part of Hanoi. At that point I had flown seventy-two combat missions over South Vietnam, North Vietnam, Laos and Cambodia since my assignment to Cam Ranh Bay in November of 1966.

I was one of twelve pilots in the flight. We received a thorough briefing on the mission and the flight took off at

3:00 PM local time. It was Friday, May 12, 1967 and I was in an F-4 Phantom flying my seventy-third mission which would take me to Hanoi for the first time.

We proceeded to a rendezvous point with a KC-135 tanker aircraft over Laos. After all of the fighters completed their refueling, our flight joined up with eighteen other aircraft loaded with bombs. The target was a boat manufacturing plant in the southwest edge of Hanoi.

Some of our aircraft were equipped with 600-gallon auxiliary fuel tanks mounted on the centerline and we were authorized to jettison them as we crossed the Black River. Eliminating the excess weight would tilt the scale of advantage our way if we had an opportunity to engage the MIGS in a dog fight.

Our first eight aircraft were carrying anti-personnel bombs for use against the gun and missile crews in the immediate vicinity of the target. The next eight were F-105 aircraft, each carrying one 3,000 pound bomb. Last in the wave of airplanes were four F-4 Phantoms. Two of them were equipped with externally mounted gun pods, an innovation that was born of necessity to increase firepower. The other two F-4's had a standard configuration of eight short range air-to-air missiles, four Sidewinders and four Sparrows.

The early model F-4 aircraft was designed for the U.S. Navy and was intended solely as a weapon to protect an aircraft carrier and its fleet of supporting vessels. It carried heat seeking Sidewinders and radar guided Sparrow missiles. It was not designed as a fighter for doing close-in dog fights. We knew we needed a way to deal with the MIGS if they chose to close in and fight. Following us was another wave of sixteen F-105's and four more F-4's.

Our flight groupings of four F-4's each were spaced five- hundred to seven-hundred feet apart, forty to fifty feet laterally. This allowed pilots and crew maximum visibility to search for enemy aircraft and for surface-to-air missiles (SAMs) that would be coming up to greet us as we approached our target at the southwest edge of Hanoi. We were flying five hundred knots indicated airspeed and maintaining an altitude of 14,000 feet.

The puffy white cumulous clouds were widely scattered and seemed to float along lazily, almost peacefully, unmindful of the forces of destruction that zoomed by them. We could see a rain shower in the distance, normal for a North Vietnamese late afternoon in May. The shower would not interfere with our mission. It could, however, create problems for the Navy strike force as they approached the target from the south/southeast.

We had been told in our briefing that on this particular day the North Vietnamese would be faced with a dilemma as to how many of their fighters they would commit to attack our force. A strike force of our naval aviators was also headed to Hanoi from the Gulf of Tonkin to bomb the same target about five minutes behind us. We were informed that the North Vietnamese Air Force had a limited number of serviceable aircraft and an insufficient number of combat-trained pilots to fly them.

Our strike force was about to cross the Black River west of Hanoi. Air Force intelligence officers had warned us that by the time we reached the river, the North Vietnamese air defense network would be active, so we knew that it was about time for the flak from anti-aircraft guns to start hacking away at us. We also knew that we could expect them to scramble their Soviet built MIG-17 and MIG-21 jet fighter aircraft to intercept our strike force.

As we crossed the Black River we began to spot minute grayish white puffs of smoke ahead and to the left of our flight path, our first indication of North Vietnamese air defense activity. The flak was coming at us. I could feel my pulse quicken. I had been an enemy target many times before and I knew the devastation an 85 millimeter shell could do to an airplane. However, I could see no need to move the aircraft about in the sky unless the bursts got a little closer.

Suddenly, the aircraft alarms sounded and we realized that we were being tracked by radar from a SAM launching site. The radio blared as one of the pilots in the strike force called out that a missile was launched. As the missile left the launch site, a huge donut-shaped cloud of smoke and dust rose into the air. The missile was tracking us. I was concerned for the pilots and crew of the rest of the squadron, as I am sure they were for us, as we desperately searched the sky for the telephone pole sized missile rushing toward our flight group at two and a half times the speed of sound.

Other missiles were launched, some following a radar signal from the ground and others blindly hoping to lock onto one of our aircraft. I felt a momentary feeling of desperation because neither I nor Lieutenant Jim Jefferson, who was in the back seat, had spotted any of the missiles. It's that feeling of "it's the one you don't see that will blast you out of the sky." I let out a sigh of relief when I saw the first missile pass overhead and explode well out to the side of us.

Normally it is easy to spot one of the missiles as it searches for a target. It moves through the air like a snake slithering lazily side to side through the water. As it is for the prey of a snake, it is much more difficult for the target to see a missile that has locked onto it. When it is coming directly at you, it is only twelve inches wide in a vast sky as it approaches.

We were fortunate as several missiles passed above our flight group and exploded when they did not find a target. One came close as it detonated before reaching us leaving a massive reddish grey fireball of forty or fifty feet. I did not realize it at the time, but some of the debris from the missile was ingested into my left engine intake.

As we approached the point where the F-105's were to

start their dive bomb run, we could understand why our intelligence officers described Hanoi as the most heavily defended city in the world. It seemed that everyone and his brother in Hanoi had a gun on this twelfth day of May, 1967, and they were all aimed at us. While the flak was intense, it was rather inaccurate. The missiles also seemed inaccurate on this mission.

By now, the first two flights of flak suppression aircraft were on their dive bombing runs. Diving at a forty-five degree angle, they quickly accelerated to 600 knots as the pilots released their ordinance simultaneously and began a four to five "G" pull up to their egress altitude. As they did so, one of the pilots spotted three MIG aircraft maneuvering into position below them. The MIG pilots preferred not to attack our airplanes unless they could spot one that already had battle damage. In that circumstance, they would attack the damaged airplane and force the crew to bail out and be captured or killed.

Once the MIG pilots entered the fracas it was time for us to go to work. Our mission was to protect the bombing aircraft. They could not maneuver well when they were heavily loaded. One of the favorite tactics of a MIG pilot was to fake an attack against the strike force before it reached its target and force the pilots to drop their ordinance on something other than the primary target. When they used this tactic, however, the North Vietnamese could not continue to shoot at the strike force for fear of downing their MIG pilots. To our good fortune, they had made that costly error before.

Our secondary mission was to provide safe passage for any of our damaged airplanes until they left North Vietnamese airspace and to provide cover for our pilots and crew who were forced to eject from their airplanes. Second only in disappointment to seeing our people fail to eject from a destroyed aircraft was seeing their parachutes slowly lowering them into enemy hands.

The radio call telling us that the MIG pilots were starting to attack our airplanes caused my adrenalin to start pumping. My heart rate increased and I was overcome by both excitement and fear. I had trained all through my career to prepare me for air-to-air battle with an enemy pilot. This would be my first opportunity to make use of that training.

My primary responsibility was to protect our element leader, Colonel Frederick "Boots" Blesse. As one of our most experienced combat pilots, Boots was an old hand at this dog fighting game. He had done battle with MIGS many times in Korea and was credited with shooting down ten of their pilots. He was shrewd, persistent and possessed all of the qualities that make an outstanding combat leader. I was proud and fortunate to be on my first air-to-air combat engagement with him. We had known each other for several years and had most recently reconnected while attending the National War College in Washington, D.C.

We spotted three MIG-17's coming down at us from

above. We started to descend to close the distance between our aircraft. As we passed through 7,000 feet, I observed that our airspeed was 700 knots as we closed in on the MIGS. Without any warning, the left afterburner that had sucked in debris earlier flamed out and I began to drop back from the rest of the flight group. I felt a terrible sense of helplessness as I tried in vain to get the afterburner to relight. Major Bob Dilger, the flight leader, radioed instructions for me to close it up. Having only my right afterburner it was impossible to follow his order. I had never felt more vulnerable.

The MIG pilots split their flight into an element of two and one, meaning one MIG separated off from the other two. Radio chatter was becoming excessive so Bob Dilger called for a channel change. He then instructed us to split our flight into two elements of two F-4's each so we could engage the MIGS. I dropped behind Boots Blesse in my crippled aircraft and armed my missile switches so that I could offer him whatever protection I could.

I had just passed through 4,000 feet when my left engine exploded. Fire warning lights came on and the airplane began a slight vibration. I tried to radio Boots that I had severe problems and would not be able to stay with him but my radio was damaged from the explosion and he was not aware that I was in trouble. The Gulf of Tonkin was twenty-five miles away, my airplane was on fire and I had lost communication with my leader. My mind raced through our pre-flight plan for an emergency of this kind which was to get out over water to be picked up by our rescue forces.

Jim Jefferson and I were still able to communicate over our internal microphones. As I turned to a southeasterly heading to try to head for water, he excitedly announced that one of the MIG pilots was coming in to attack us. He could see the smoke and fire coming from our airplane. I felt like a sitting duck. When the MIG was in range of 2,000 feet of us, he opened fire with his cannon. He was apparently inexperienced because he was shooting behind me. I banked hard to the left as my airspeed and altitude continued to dissipate.

Jim anxiously reminded me that we were getting too low. We were down to about 350 knots airspeed and it was all I could do to try to evade the MIG while maintaining control. Suddenly, I felt the airplane shudder and then go out of control. I felt myself in a negative "G" condition with my head pushed up against the canopy. The control stick was vibrating violently and the aircraft suddenly went to the full nose down position. The vibration began to beat against my left leg so severely that I could not overcome the control pressures to manage any degree of maneuverability.

The aircraft, now completely out of control, began to tumble through the air end over end. I shouted for Jim to get out and within seconds I heard a loud explosion behind me so I assumed that he had ejected. I tried to get my body positioned properly to eject but the forces of gravity were working against me. I managed to get one hand above my head to pull the ejection curtain but resistance kept me from getting my other hand up. I had no choice but to use the "D" ring between my knees. That also proved easier said than done because I was being tossed about so badly that I could not get my second hand on the ring. I mustered all of the will I had and managed to get a firm grip on the ring with my left hand and give it a hard yank. The canopy blew and in an instant my seat followed

As I catapulted out, I consciously closed my eyes and held tightly to the D ring. Though only seconds passed, it felt like an eternity before I could force myself to open my eyes. When I did, it was just in time to see my airplane pass above my left shoulder in a steep dive. Fire engulfed it from the cockpits to the tail. I was below safe ejection altitude and stood a very good chance of major injury from ground impact.

As I drifted down in my parachute, a thousand thoughts ran helter-skelter through my mind. My right arm seemed seriously injured and was bleeding profusely. I had evidently been hit by some part of the airplane during ejection. My thoughts flashed to my family and I wondered if I would ever see or speak to them again. This was the Friday before Mother's Day and I had mailed cards to my wife and mother from Da Nang that morning. Before those cards would arrive, I thought, someone would deliver a much dreaded message about my fate as either a prisoner or worse.

The ground rapidly approached and I began to fearfully wonder what was about to happen to me. I knew capture was inevitable upon parachuting into North Vietnamese territory, especially so near Hanoi. Even though an air war was still in process above and anti-aircraft guns and missiles were being fired and exploding all around, I slipped into a netherworld of silent consciousness. Dozens of thoughts and questions raced through my mind.

I reckoned I would spend the next two years in a communist prison. I envisioned that America would continue the bombing for another year to force the North Vietnamese to the negotiating table; then it would take another year for the negotiations to get results so we could be released. My thoughts turned to concern for Jim Jefferson. I hoped that he had survived the ejection and had managed to parachute safely down.

Then reality set in. I turned my attention to my injured right arm. My flight suit was torn and bloody. My first thought was that my arm had been severed as I ejected. I looked down and much to my relief saw that my arm was still in place and that my fingers were still working when I wiggled them. I realized I was probably experiencing shock since my mind was slow to process my priorities.

It suddenly hit me that I needed to contact my flight and let them know I was alive. I had on an emergency survival vest which included a radio, a 38 caliber pistol with one hundred rounds of ammo, a first aid kit, a mirror to signal search and rescue aircraft and a fishing kit. I had two baby bottles filled with drinking water in my "G" suit pocket.

I pulled out my radio to call my flight leader but realized I did not have time before landing. I looked below me and saw flashes of gun fire. The North Vietnamese were shooting at me as I descended. There was so much ruckus going on with missile and anti-aircraft explosions that I had not heard the recoil from the small weapons fire. Now the thoughts racing through my mind turned from an expectation that they would want to capture and incarcerate me to the realization that they wanted to kill me.

I quickly pushed the antenna back down on my survival radio and put it in my vest pocket just before I touched the ground. I saw that I would land in a dry rice paddy and steeled myself for the impact. I landed okay and rolled onto my right side as I was trained to do in survival school. I regained a standing position and released the shroud lines on my parachute to prevent being dragged across the rice paddy. I immediately crouched down and took out my survival radio. I called "Dagger Flight" and advised that "*Dagger Four is OK.*" In my excitement, I forgot to tell them that Jim Jefferson had ejected before I did. I should have reported "Dagger Four-One is OK" and "Dagger Four-Two ejected but status unknown."

I returned the radio to my pocket and instinctively began to reach for my pistol but realized halfway through the motion that North Vietnamese army troops were all around me in the rice paddy and threateningly coming toward me, all of their weapons pointed in my direction. In the brief time that I had been on the ground, they had not fired shots at me, so my better judgment told me it would be futile to try to avoid capture. Even in my fear, I suddenly became aware of the extreme heat on the hard packed dry rice paddy. It must have been over one hundred degrees. As the soldiers circled in close, I raised my hands in surrender and waited for the worst to happen.

# Chapter 3

During my twenty years in military service, many of my friends and acquaintances had been shot down and held prisoner or worse, killed in action. Being an eternal optimist, I believed that I would never be shot down and captured. Yet, here I was about to become a prisoner of war, the most terrifying thing imaginable to a pilot, especially one who was forty-three years old and far along in my career.

As a full colonel, I knew that I would likely be considered a prize capture for the people who were coming for me. I was suddenly devastated by thoughts of spending months and perhaps years in a dirty, stinking prison deprived of even the most basic necessities of life. I began to doubt my optimistic thoughts that I could expect a one to two year incarceration followed by a negotiated release. Maybe the easier option would have been to draw my pistol and die honorably and if lucky, taking one or two of them with me.

The apparent officer-in-charge of the enemy patrol approached me, drew his pistol and pointed it at me. My heart sank. I could see that he was even more nervous than me, if that was possible. The hand holding his pistol was shaking like a leaf. I continued to hold my hands in the air as he glared at me, letting me know that I was not to move.

His troops moved in and proceeded to strip me of all of my gear and personal possessions. One soldier excitedly scraped the cheap Seiko watch from my wrist. Fortunately, I had left my Omega watch, my Air Force ring and my wedding band in my trailer at Cam Ranh Bay. I could see they considered my pistol and ammunition to be a trophy prize along with my survival vest. They seemed a little confused when they pulled out the two baby bottles filled with water.

Next came the stripping. They ordered me to remove my flight suit and combat boots that I noticed quickly disappeared as they were confiscated by the soldiers closest to me. I had always heard what a dreaded experience hazing was for young men joining fraternities or sports teams. I now understood the humiliation and embarrassment they endured. There is no more helpless feeling than being naked and vulnerable while knowing there is nothing you can do about it.

I must have been an amusing sight to the soldiers as I stood surrounded, transfixed, in my boxer shorts that were decorated with large red crabs printed all over them. Fruit of the Loom would have been proud.

The officer directed his troops to tie my arms behind me with a piece of the nylon they gathered from my parachute. As they secured my arms behind me, I looked skyward and saw that a serious air battle was still in process. The Navy strike force was attacking the same boat factory that was the target we had just bombed.

The officer pointed to a grove of bamboo about a quarter of a mile away and motioned for me to start trotting toward it. Despite my age, I was in good physical condition. I had averaged about one hundred and fifty-five pounds for the last fifteen years. My right elbow, injured during ejection, bothered me as I ran barefooted toward the bamboo thicket. I had about an eight inch cut that was bleeding, but not excessively. I knew we were headed toward the bamboo to hide from our airplanes still flying overhead, but there was nothing I could do to avoid it. Those were my guys up there who I knew wanted to save me. I felt a momentary pang of guilt knowing the desperation they would feel for failing me.

Once we reached the bamboo thicket, we hunkered down to avoid detection. When it appeared to the officer that the airplanes had left the area, they wrapped my flight suit around my head to use as a blindfold. They pushed and pulled me stumbling along. I could feel from the dirt worn smooth from foot traffic that we were on a rice paddy dike between paddies. I struggled to stay upright as I blindly stumbled along for several hundred yards until I finally tumbled into a ditch. The people in charge of me shouted and yelled instructions to each other and finally got me back on top of the dike and moving again.

We arrived at a rocky roadway after what felt like an

eternity. I immediately missed my boots. The trek through the hot and dry rice paddy, then along the paddy dike path, had taken its toll on my bare feet. The roadway we now encountered was brutal on my tender feet. There was a purpose to their taking away my boots. They knew I could not possibly run away from them now.

We crossed a wooden bridge and walked a few hundred feet. I began to hear the excited-sounding voices of women and children. Being blindfolded was terribly disorienting. I could not tell whether they were reacting to my presence or my colorful boxer shorts. I did not imagine that they had seen many American pilots, especially not clad in atrocious red and white underwear. Nevertheless, they did not harm me in any way.

We crossed back over the bridge and walked a few hundred yards to a large depression in the ground. I presumed the initial detour over the bridge was to allow my captors to celebrate by parading their prisoner for villagers to see. They shoved me to the ground and made it clear they wanted me to stay put.

After thirty to forty minutes I was becoming anxious when I heard a truck approaching. It stopped and its engine turned off. I could hear a number of soldiers gathered close by. Finally, I felt them tugging at me to get up off of the ground.

They led me to the back of the truck and yanked and pushed at me to get me to climb up into the truck bed. It was awkward and painful as I tried to climb over the steel gate with my hands still tied and my injured right arm aching. After a couple of difficult failed attempts to mount the truck with them punching and prodding at me, I lost my temper and yelled at them. "You bunch of dumb bastards," I shouted. "If you would take this blindfold off so I could see, I would try to do what you want."

Much to my surprise, they removed the flight suit from around my head. I did not know whether it was because they understood my English or just managed to read my gestures. It took a few seconds for my vision to focus in the bright sunlight. I could now see that this was an army truck similar to our two and one-half-ton troop trucks.

The depression in the ground turned out to be an abandoned anti-aircraft gun emplacement. The people in the village across the bridge from where I now stood were still gathered around peering and pointing in my direction. I was relieved that they were curious rather than furious at someone who was bombing their country.

Once again the soldiers signaled for me to mount the truck. I awkwardly put my foot on the bumper rail and pushed myself up so my stomach was on the floor of the truck. I rolled to a sitting position and managed to stand as they pushed me forward and motioned for me to sit with my back against the cab. The officer with the pistol and two of his people got into the truck bed with me. I now had a panoramic view out the back of the truck as we moved slowly away, with the rest of the soldiers and the villagers staring after us.

We had traveled a couple of miles when the odor of my burning aircraft struck me. Shortly, the truck turned off of the road and pulled into an open field and stopped. The officer and one of the guards climbed out the back and left with several other soldiers who were waiting for them.

A cluster of curious villagers gathered at the back of the truck and pointed at me, excitedly chattering to each other. At first, I did not sense any hostility from the crowd. It was more an atmosphere of curiosity about the strange looking, half naked American. All at once a young Vietnamese civilian ran and jumped on the back of the truck and started for me threateningly. He appeared distraught and angry, intent on attacking me. But the soldier guarding me stood between us and butted him on the shoulder with his rifle, ordering him to get off of the truck. Thankfully, he followed the order and dejectedly climbed down.

I nervously sat and waited for what would happen next. In about thirty minutes the officer and my other guard returned. I saw that they carried items with them that appeared to be taken from our flight. I was getting anxious to learn what had happened to Jim Jefferson so I got up and walked toward the officer pleading with him to tell me what he knew. This did not go as well as I hoped as he put his pistol to my forehead and directed me to sit back down where I was. Although I had received no training in the language, I immediately began to understand Vietnamese. He had gotten braver and more authoritative since our initial meeting and made it clear to me that he would not tolerate any unusual action from me. I pleaded for information about Jim Jefferson, miming my query as best I could, but they did not seem to understand, or at least did not want me to think they did. However, I saw that they had Jim's name tag which had been cut from his flight suit, a knee held clip board that would contain our flight information and what appeared to be Jim's flight helmet.

I was greatly distressed that they did not bring him to the truck. If they had these items that belonged to him, they had to have either been taken from him personally or from his body. I did not want to believe the latter. My mind raced with assumptions. He could be badly injured and unable to travel and the bastards might have left him to die. Or, perhaps a medical truck took him away for treatment. But that did not make much sense because my guards had his personal effects.

I knew we were at a low altitude in an uncontrolled situation when Jim ejected. Statistically, major injuries or death occur eighty-five percent of the time when ejecting from an F-4 Phantom in those conditions. Jim could have had an arm or leg mangled during ejection and died from loss of blood. Or, he could have suffered a blunt trauma head injury as he was being tossed around.

Then, I remembered that soldiers on the ground were firing at me as I floated down in my parachute and knew that I had considered using my pistol to defend myself. I then thought that perhaps the enemy shot Jim either in his parachute aloft or when he tried to escape and fight back on the ground. I just hoped he took some of them with him if that was the case. I secretly held out hope that he was injured and would be brought to the POW camp later. I desperately wanted to see him alive again.

We started to move forward in the truck very slowly until we were back on the rocky road. The driver then accelerated to about twenty-five or thirty miles per hour. We had driven a few miles when I began to assess my situation. With my background at the Pentagon and later as a student at the National War College, I had been privy to a lot of highly sensitive security information. I was not in an enviable position, especially given that I was, at full Colonel, the senior ranking American Air Force pilot to be captured in North Vietnam.

I considered lying to my captors by telling them that I was a Major or Lieutenant Colonel. But, then I realized that I had a Geneva Convention card that listed my rank as full Colonel. I thought about trying to hide or destroy the card. However, since they had taken all of my possessions except my colorful underwear, they would already have the card. Chances are they had probably already acquired intelligence about me as well as many other senior officers assigned to units in South Vietnam and Thailand. I realized the futility of trying to deceive them about my rank and decided to discard that misguided idea.

As the truck rumbled along the rough gravel road, I closed my eyes and forced myself, in this my worst experience of adversity, to take pause and call on God to ask for strength, courage and guidance. I repeated the Lord's Prayer and the Twenty-Third Psalm. It came naturally to me and was not a spur of the moment decision. I had been a Christian for many years and called on Him often.

I opened my eyes and turned my attention back to the events as they unfolded. My years of military and navigational training taught me to be observant of my surroundings and always try to remain aware of my whereabouts and make mental notes of the things I saw. I noted that our general direction of travel was toward the southeast. I spotted approximately ten petroleum tanks along our route through the countryside that appeared to be capable of holding thousands of gallons of fuel. They had made no attempt to hide them nor were they camouflaged in any way. Our intelligence officers would love to have that information, I thought.

I found myself dreading the dark as the sun began its decent over the western horizon. I had no control over my circumstance but at least the daylight allowed me to be aware of my surroundings. Once dusk settled, I knew I would be moved about blindly and I found that prospect frightening. I was not typically afraid of the dark but knew I could get that way if my captors decided to mistreat me as I suspected they eventually would.

Soon we reached a paved road and turned toward the north-northeast. The flow of military trucks and light vehicles began to increase as we reached an urban area spotted with large buildings. I could hear frenzied commotion ahead of us as we slowed to a near crawl and then stopped. The dank odor and sting of smoke from burning buildings attacked my nose and eyes. The alarming sound of sirens and bells were everywhere. Panicked yelling and screaming surrounded us. People were running with buckets of water trying to extinguish the fires caused by our bombing.

My guards, who were in the back of the truck with me, began yelling to passing people and pointing me out to them. No doubt they were bragging at having captured one of the pilots responsible for the death and destruction that rained down from above. The citizens of Hanoi, curious to see what one of us looked like, trotted along with the truck as we slowly started to move again.

We began to increase speed as we moved away from the bomb damaged area, leaving the Vietnamese residents behind. The truck wove through the suburbs of Hanoi making abrupt right and left turns. My hands were still tied behind my back and I was having a hard time maintaining my balance. I kept trying to use my feet to sustain myself but they were so tender that I could not gain traction on the truck bed. I kept falling helplessly from side to side. My injured right arm banged against the hard surface of the truck bed each time I got off balance and my back was getting sore from rubbing against the forward frame of the bed as the truck bounced and swerved.

To my surprise, one of the guards stood up and came from the rear of the truck and placed his hand on my shoulder to steady me. In doing so, he took notice of my bloody slashed elbow. Showing me unexpected compassion, he removed a compress from his military issue first-aid kit and bandaged my wound. His humane actions gave me hope that what lay ahead for me might not be as horrible as I expected.

As darkness enveloped us, our driver maneuvered the truck into a compound that I assumed to be a prison. I managed to catch a glimpse of a clock on one of the buildings and noted it read 8:45. My guards once again used my flight suit to blindfold me as we pulled to a stop.

I heard muffled talking and the beat of footsteps from people approaching the truck. I could feel their presence when they were directly behind the truck only a few feet from me. A man speaking perfect English asked for my name, rank, serial number and date of birth. I considered objecting to the questioning but then realized that the information he was seeking was included on my Geneva Convention card that was now in their possession, so I responded with the accurate information.

Without further questioning, he left and our driver cranked the engine, backed up and pulled out onto the hard surface roadway again. We drove through the outskirts of Hanoi as best I could tell, but with the blindfold I could not tell direction and had difficulty staying oriented. When we stopped again, one of the guards removed my blindfold. It was now fully dark.

Behind the truck I could see a three-story building. It was surrounded by a high wall and I could see bars on the windows. A crowd was gathered. In any other circumstance it would have seemed like a planned reception, but these people rapidly became agitated. A couple of them tried to get into the back of the truck, intent on attacking me, but the guards pushed them back with their rifles.

A young woman with flowing black hair climbed onto the side running board, pulled back the canvas and began to hit me over the head with a large flashlight. The guards furiously forced her to back away. The driver and officer finally returned from the building, climbed into the truck and quickly drove away to escape the mob of angry Vietnamese. My guards efficiently placed my flight suit over my head to serve as a blindfold once again.

We were moving at a much faster speed than we had traveled up to now as if urgently needing to get somewhere. We passed only a few other vehicles and I could see the glare of their headlights rising and then drifting away into the darkness through the material of my blindfold. In a few minutes the truck slowed and came to an abrupt stop. I could hear loud and excited Vietnamese chatter, then rattling chains followed by the unmistakable sound of large iron gates swinging open. The driver pulled carefully through the now open gates and stopped. My guards removed the blindfold and I watched, terrified, as soldiers slowly and methodically closed and chained the gates.

In that traumatic moment I knew that those locked gates represented my total and complete loss of freedom. There was no escape, no turning back. This was not a dream. I was fully awake and had to face the fact that I had been trying to avoid. I was now a prisoner of war in a formidable old French prison in North Vietnam.

I subsequently learned that my new living hell was named Hoa Lo (one translation is "fiery furnace"), which had been nicknamed "The Hanoi Hilton" by prior American prisoners. While it isn't known who originally gave it this name, it is believed to be first put in writing in 1965 when POW Bob Shumaker etched "Welcome to the Hanoi Hilton" on a bucket handle to greet the arrival of new POW Robert Peel.

# Chapter 4

The guards motioned for me to get up and move to the rear of the truck. I awkwardly leaned forward to stand and caught a glance of my boots that were taken from me when I was captured. They were in the front corner of the bed. I instinctively reached down to grasp them, hoping I would be allowed to keep them along with my flight suit that they kept tying over my head and eyes. I managed to touch the hard leather toe of one boot before the guard who had shown me compassion earlier shouted at me in a scornful voice and signaled threateningly with his rifle to leave the boots where they were. Perhaps he wanted to keep them as a souvenir or even to wear, although I could see that they were too large for him. I badly wanted to keep them, I guess to cling to some personal item, perhaps as my link to the outside world. What a haunting feeling to voice the words "outside world" in my head.

Terrifying thoughts raced through my mind. How long would I be a prisoner? Would I survive this ordeal? What kind of treatment was I facing? Regrettably, my last question was about to be brutally answered.

The guards pushed me out the back of the truck and I awkwardly fell to the ground. I got to my knees and managed to stand and look around. I was in a courtyard that was about sixty or seventy feet wide and two hundred feet long. A wide driveway ran down the center bordered by raised flower beds that were eighteen to twenty inches high. A grape arbor eerily shadowed the entire courtyard. I could see several low wattage light bulbs that cast odd profiles as people moved about, seemingly unconcerned about the drama unfolding in front of them at the main gate to the prison.

A guard who was taller than the others moved in behind me and pushed my head down with his open hand. I defensively reared my head back up, anxious to see what would happen next. Other guards circled in around like geese following the head goose. They carried long rifles that were nearly as tall as they were.

Someone started pushing me from behind using the butt of his rifle as a prod, forcing me to walk in a big circle. As I stumbled along, the gaggle of guards who were now cackling like geese started punching and slapping me in the head and forcing me to bow down. When I resisted by trying to raise my head, the beatings intensified.

The scene oddly reminded me of a paddle line for a fraternity initiation ceremony. It seemed like a stupid thought, but I found myself feeling pity for the underclassmen who endured such hazing. My mind was shocked back to my present predicament when a guard kidney-punched me with the butt of his rifle. Seeing the obvious pain this caused, the others joined in the fun and repeatedly butted my kidneys, hips and thighs. And, each time I tried to raise my head they beat it back down again with their hands and fists.

I managed to glance out the side of my eye to see that a crowd of people had gathered to watch the show. One old lady who seemed bored as if she was seeing a repeat performance nonchalantly squatted, thighs on calves, and brushed at her betel nut stained teeth with her forefinger. The guards were dancing around her as if they were in a tribal ritual, shouting what appeared to be Vietnamese obscenities at me and signaling for me to bow in sorrow to them.

The beating was excruciatingly painful. As I began to slip into a state of shock, my body started to resist by feeling numb to the blows. This gave me newfound strength and I set my determination to resist any way that I could. I would not allow these jerks to intimidate me. It was my first battle with them and I was determined to win it.

Time after time they beat me to my knees, but each time I would manage to regain my feet and continue walking in a circle. I started to see bright flashes of light and thought I must be starting to hallucinate. Then I realized there were photographers snapping pictures of me from their positions in the crowd. I stopped walking long enough to shout at them. "I hope you will show these pictures to the whole world so they will know that you are a bunch of no good bastards," I yelled.

Surprisingly, the beating stopped. Two guards took me by the elbows and led me across the courtyard and through an open doorway to what I would come to recognize as an interrogation room where we paused to wait, for what I was not sure. I took this opportunity to survey the room. It was approximately twenty-five feet square with what I guessed was a twelve-foot high ceiling. Two wooden French doors opened into the courtyard. The glass for the windows in the doors was broken out and replaced with six vertical iron bars in each. The openings were covered with dark blue cloth. The floor was covered with twelve-inch terra cotta tiles, some broken loose from the cement. The floor was in disrepair where tiles were loose and had been moved around.

Near the back of the room was a long table covered by the same blue cloth as was used to cover the windows and bars that were mounted in the upper door panels. The cloth flowed to the floor on all sides. Three plain kitchen-type wooden chairs were neatly arranged behind the table. A short wooden stool sat in front of the table intentionally positioned much lower than the seat height of the chairs. I instinctively knew that I would become too familiar with that stool. They had demanded that I bow to them and would now force me to subservience by seating me well below my captors.

The guards released their grip on my arms and promptly left through the open French doors, closing and latching them carefully. I was alone for the first time since my capture. I searched around the room for a potential avenue of escape, knowing all along that it was a futile effort.

As I surveyed the cloth covered table I wondered if there would be tools for torture or other revealing devices hidden underneath. There had to be a reason for the cloth covering that draped to the floor. I decided it was worth the risk to investigate and walked over to the table and lifted the skirt. I expected to find something underneath, if not torture devices, then recording equipment. To my surprise, the view under the table was just more blue cloth from the other side.

I did not want my captors to think I was snooping around, so I walked back to the center of the room where they had left me. It wasn't that I wanted them to think I would be obedient. I was just trying not to antagonize them into becoming angry and putting me through the torturous treatment I had received before they brought me into this room.

It is strange how your body responds to adversity. I had gone more than seven hours without water and just now began to notice that my tongue felt like it was coated with cotton. I then began to check myself and recognized the beginning signs of dehydration. My kidneys were hurting. I needed to urinate badly, but I was not sure if the urge was from the lower back beating I had taken.

I looked down at my bare legs. There was something

other than just my colorful underwear that made me feel a need to cover them. My nudity had made me feel vulnerable since my capture, but something about my bare legs added another dimension. I realized that if I had pants on it would give me a sense of manhood that I now knew they were trying to take away. I also became aware that I had serious body odor. The deodorant I had applied this morning before takeoff had definitely worn off.

Less than five minutes passed before a Vietnamese man, small of stature and who appeared to be in his early forties, authoritatively marched through the French doors. He informed me, in broken but somewhat understandable English, that he was the camp political officer and since I was captured in his country, I was not a prisoner of war but instead a war criminal. As such, I would be tried by a military court.

I tried to process what that meant to me. One facet of survival training suddenly came to mind: Following World War II, an International Convention convened in Geneva, Switzerland and outlawed cruel and inhumane treatment of prisoners and/or detainees. Most nations agreed to recognize and abide by the Treaty, but I knew that the North Vietnamese had not and would not treat us as prisoners of war.

I interpreted his words as confirming my belief that they would not be honoring the normal Geneva Convention rules. Would I be subjected to a communist court that would unilaterally find me guilty and put me in front of a firing squad or, worse yet, to be hanged by the neck until dead? I thought I was a brave American, but this was becoming a serious test of my bravado.

The political officer showed irritation that I did not immediately respond to his statement of how I would be treated. He angrily shouted that, as part of camp regulations, I must show proper respect to all Vietnamese including bowing down to them any time I was in their presence. He instructed me never to try to communicate with the other prisoners who, like me, were also criminals.

He faced to one side while speaking to me and I noticed that his left eye sort of bugged out when viewed from where I stood and seemed to rotate slowly from side to side. I made a mental note to nickname him "Bug" so I would remember who he was in the future. I was determined not to show emotion or fear and did my best to reflect total indifference to his spiel.

I could see that he was beginning to lose his temper when his left eye rotated faster and faster as he spoke. His exasperation showing, he angrily turned to walk from the room and informed me that three officials would arrive shortly to ask me some questions. His parting threat was that I would be wise to answer them.

Alone again for the second time, I attempted to gather and organize my thoughts. I was keenly aware that Bug was just the first wave of an interrogation I feared would turn to torture. I was determined to steel myself against breaking, no matter what the cost.

Only a few minutes passed before three men dressed in green military shirts and slacks marched into the room single file, apparently wanting to impress me with how official they appeared. The first two reminded me of the ARVN soldiers I had come in contact with in South Vietnam, slight of build and perhaps five and a half feet tall. I guessed them to be in their thirties or early forties. The third, however, was a few inches taller with a stocky build and close cropped hair on a head that was larger and rounder than the others. I guessed his age to be perhaps fifty and estimated his weight to be around one hundred and fifty to one hundred and fifty-five pounds. I was not sure whether he was Vietnamese and thought he might be Chinese.

One of the smaller men instructed me to sit on the stool and face them as they took their seats behind the cloth covered table, staring down on me. He and the other one who was clearly Vietnamese began the questioning. They each had small books they removed from their shirt pockets that they used to take notes of my responses to their interrogation. I felt somewhat relieved when they began by asking for my name, rank, serial number and date of birth, questions to which I knew they already had answers and standard under rules of the Geneva Convention of 1954.

Next they demanded that I tell them about my military unit, which base I was from and what kind of aircraft I was flying. I refused to answer, instead repeating my name, rank, serial number and date of birth repeatedly. Then they began asking me for details about my family and my personal life, whether I was married, had children and if so whether boys or girls and their ages. I continued to refuse to respond other than to provide the required information under the Convention. I told them that no matter how many times they asked, I would not answer questions that went beyond the requirements of the Geneva Convention.

This clearly raised their ire and they stood above me, shaking their fists and shouting that I was a murderer of innocent men, women, children and old people. With their anger came threats that they would get the information they wanted violently if I continued to refuse to cooperate, but still I sternly declined.

The three of them abruptly marched out of the room and sent "Bug", the camp political officer, back to try to reason with me. Bug was clearly irritated with me, his darting eyes revealing his anxiety. His tact suddenly changed as he calmly informed me that if I would only cooperate, I would avoid harsher treatment and could enjoy better living conditions and even be able to write to my family.

I reminded him that the Convention specified that I would be allowed to write one seven-line letter every month. I informed him that my family had nothing to do with the war and that I would never cooperate with them even if I was not allowed to write letters. To me, cooperate meant collaborate and I would never disgrace myself, my country or the Air Force by collaborating with the enemy.

I could see that all of my actions up to now had served only to intensify his agitation. He shrugged as if to indicate he understood that I had planted my feet. The "carrot" approach had failed and I feared and expected that the "stick" approach would follow. Bug hurriedly left the room, shaking his head in dismay.

As soon as the door closed behind Bug, it was opened again by a slightly built Vietnamese guard who motioned for me to follow him. He was impatient and instructed me to move "quigly." I could not help but notice how much he, especially his eyes, reminded me of a pig.

"Pigeye" led me to an adjacent room that we entered through a single wooden doorway. He carried a small bundle of clothing that he tossed out onto the floor in the center of the room and I could see that they were a short sleeved undershirt and boxer style undershorts. The top was a black tee shirt and the black boxers had a draw string around the waist. He motioned for me to pick them up and put them on as he left me alone in the room.

I wondered what would happen to my colorful shorts I had to remove to adorn the ugly black ones. The rough fabric chafed against my now tender skin as I put them on. It did not help that I was filthy and stinking from the day's events. At the same time, I felt relieved to have more of my body covered in the presence of my enemies even though the cheap black garments were psychologically depressing and another tool I was sure they would use to demean me.

The effects of dehydration began to consume me. My tongue felt like a rolled-up cotton rag that did not belong in my mouth. My lips were dry and severely chapped. My lower back was sore to the touch and my kidneys ached. I remembered talking to other pilots who had, for various reasons, been forced to bail out of their airplanes and immediate dry mouth and thirst were common among them as symptoms of the initial trauma. One friend joked after his experience that he could not understand why anyone would want to jump out of a perfectly good airplane. I guessed it was now seven or eight hours since I ejected and a couple of hours before that since I had a drink of water.

My thoughts wandered again to what had become of Jim Jefferson. Did the fact that they had his name tag, helmet and other possessions prove that he had been killed? Not especially, I reasoned. They probably retained all of my stuff the same way. But, where was he? I felt a sudden pang of guilt that I had failed to report when I radioed to my flight group that he had bailed out earlier than me.

My mind was jumping around from one thing to the other, an effect of the severe fatigue and dehydration. I wondered when I would have to face Bug and the other interrogators again. I looked around to survey the new room I was in. Some strange looking equipment was stacked in the far corner from where I stood. On closer inspection I realized these were the tools they would use for torture. There was an eight-foot long iron bar an inch to an inch and a half thick, a set of iron leg stocks that would fit around your ankles and clamp down, ropes, handcuffs and several nylon straps.

Regardless that it was hot and humid, a cold chill consumed me and I felt my stomach begin to cramp and convulse. I felt dizzy and nauseous from fear of the pain and indignities I would soon face. I repeated to myself over and over that I had a duty to soldier up and take whatever came like a man.

I had a wealth of sensitive information to protect from my job in the Pentagon. During the early days of the Vietnam War, I helped select ninety-five strategic targets that if attacked by Air Force and Navy pilots, would cause North Vietnam to seriously consider ending the war against South Vietnam on reasonably negotiated terms. I was also privy to extremely sensitive information about the Air Force nuclear weapons stockpile and the intended targets of those weapons. It was dreadful to think that I might be tortured while being interrogated along those extremely delicate lines.

My perception of the North Vietnamese was that they did not have a good understanding of the principles of conventional warfare. I did recognize, however, that they were experts at guerrilla and urban warfare. They proved themselves in that regard when they defeated a superior French force during the battle of Dien Bien Phu in 1954.

I guessed any interest they would show in nuclear weaponry would originate with their Soviet or Chinese partners and armament suppliers. I had read intelligence reports that the Chinese supplied Chi-com hand grenades, rocket propelled grenades and other armament to the North and their Viet Cong contingent in the south. I knew there were also reports from the American forces in the field that Chinese soldiers had been observed leading or accompanying enemy columns against our ground forces. I had just been targeted and perhaps shot down by a Russian MIG and lost an engine to debris from the explosion of a SAM, so I knew the Soviets supplied aircraft, pilot training, armament and support to the North. It would be reasonable to expect that either of these would want to collect and use the names and backgrounds of the North Vietnamese captives and to direct that specific information be extorted from them. I knew I would have to find the strength to guard against that possibility.

Bug came and got me and led me back to the original interrogation room. He directed me to sit on the stool and abruptly left the room. The three interrogators immediately marched through the double doors and slammed them closed. I was relieved to be free of the room where the torture tools loomed but suspected I was far from free of the ugliness that I anticipated lay before me. Their expressions of consternation told me they were determined to extract information from me by whatever means necessary.

They began this session by painstakingly detailing the history of the war and placing the blame for it on the United States for committing aggression against a small and innocent nation. As a student of the war college and an Air Force officer, I had studied Indochina for many years. I knew the responsibility for atrocities against South Vietnam and its people lay with the Ho Chi Minh regime.

I listened intently as they tried to spin their story into a believable history. They pointed out that visitors had come in several groups from the United States and those people had expressed support for North Vietnam and its efforts at unification of the north and south. They asked if I was aware of the anti-war movement by my countrymen as expressed by my own people who had voluntarily come to show North Vietnam their support. I was not impressed by their presentation and attempt at placing blame for the war. I declined to comment or answer any of their questions.

Like a scene from an old detective movie, one of the interrogators reached into his shirt pocket and took out a pack of cigarettes. He removed an unfiltered cigarette from the pack and put it between his lips as provocatively as he knew how. He seemed to truly believe that I would be punished by some habitual craving for tobacco. He removed a lighter from his pants pocket and made a grand gesture of lighting the cigarette, taking a long drag and exhaling a stream of blue smoke in my direction.

American movies have traditionally glamorized cigarette smoking, so it was easy for him to assume that all Americans like to smoke. Little did he know that I had never smoked cigarettes, although I did take a cigar occasionally, but I never cared for the odor cigarettes left in a room or on clothing. This elementary effort at psychological warfare would have been amusing were it not for my current circumstances. Still, his gestures indicated that he assumed I would ask, or even beg, for a cigarette. I took pleasure in winning this brief mental game by ignoring his overtures.

Again, the interrogation turned to questions of a military nature. What was my target in the north? How many airplanes were in my attack group? What armament were we carrying? I repeatedly responded with my name, rank, serial number and date of birth as required. I knew that they were familiar with the rules of the Geneva Convention since they first captured Everette Alvarez in August of 1964 and more than two hundred pilots since then.

They began to show their agitation at my lack of cooperation and angrily stalked out of the room. I had a feeling things would get a whole lot worse for me before this night ended.

Shortly, Bug marched into the room and angrily shouted that I was failing to abide by camp regulations and my failure to cooperate would be met with severe punishment. He was not happy that his role as chief political officer and head negotiator was not getting the desired results. I would have to pay for making him look bad.

His spiel was interrupted as the French doors slammed open and Pigeye entered carrying the long steel bar followed by the largest Vietnamese guy I had ever seen. The big guy carried the rest of the torture equipment I had seen in the adjacent room.

These two were practiced and efficient as they began their torturous preparations. They roughly yanked my arms behind my back and placed adjustable handcuffs on my wrists. They turned the tightening ratchet which intensified the pain with each rotation. I was then pushed to the floor into a sitting position so my ankles could be forced into a pair of leg stocks. My feet were terribly swollen from the day's events and the guards stood on my legs to force them to fit into the stocks. This brutal effort tore the skin from my ankles and caused blood to flow freely.

Now that my hands and feet were immobile, they placed a nylon strap around my upper arms behind my back and both guards pulled and stretched the straps to overlap my shoulder blades. I uncontrollably groaned and yelped in response to the intense pain.

Next, they inserted the long iron bar through the leg stocks, pulled my arms up behind me and yanked the straps over my shoulders downward, forcing my head between my knees. They then tied and stretched the straps around the iron bar. My ankles stung and ached, my wrists felt like they were breaking and I was afraid my shoulders were coming out of joint. It felt like my back was about to snap and my kidneys still ached profusely from the earlier beatings. The pain was so severe that I began to hope I would lose consciousness, but I was learning that the human body can take an awful lot of punishment. It was more than I wanted to find out I could take.

I learned during survival training to tolerate torture as long as possible but to try to avoid losing my faculties. I was slowly losing the ability to think clearly and I cried out for them to release me. I knew I was reaching the twilight phase of consciousness where a person is liable to reveal information to his enemy. I was determined not to allow their abuse to take me to that threshold.

# Chapter 5

I felt myself fading into delirium as I began to see white spots and I was having difficulty focusing my vision. As my torturers moved about, it appeared that they left trailing silhouettes like shadows following them around the room. I was blessedly close to passing out.

Pigeye recognized the state I was reaching and was too smart to allow me this reprieve from my pain. They suddenly and efficiently untied the straps from the iron bar and from over my shoulders and forced me into a sitting position. While it was a great relief to get my head from between my knees, it was excruciatingly painful to unfold my body into an erect position.

My hands continued to ache as they were left bound behind my back with the ratchet still securely tightened. The tingling pins and needles sensation in my fingers told me that the bindings had cut off blood flow to my extremities. If left in this condition long enough I would be in danger of losing some or all of my fingers and possibly even my entire hands.

My eyes gradually regained focus and my ability to think clearly began to return. It was apparent that Pigeye and his cohort were trying to decide what to do with me next as they hovered over me speaking to each other in rapid Vietnamese. I considered the quandary I was in and knew I had only survived the initial phase of Torture 101. I could not give the enemy any information but, if I didn't, I would be tortured until I relented.

This torture could leave me physically disabled or even kill me, I realized. Was it worth my health or possibly my life to protect information that was readily available in American newspapers and magazines? It was a deep personal dilemma for me and I could not figure out how to deal with it.

I repeatedly asked myself "How am I going to survive this ordeal?" I did not want to compromise my principles nor did I want to give them any meaningful information of any kind.

I finally formulated what I thought would be a fail-safe plan in my mind. I would answer some of their questions with a response that would stop the torture. I needed to establish a degree of credibility so my responses, if it came to a point where I absolutely felt I had to respond, would contain an element of truth but not the whole truth.

Pigeye and the big guy I would come to know as "Buff", nicknamed so by other prisoners, picked me up by my elbows from my sitting position and sat me on the interrogation stool. The three interrogators returned to their sitting positions behind the table looking down on me.

As their questions began, I was determined to frustrate

their efforts so I pretended not to understand. I was hoping to give myself time to figure out plausible answers that would make sense to them but not really tell them anything of importance. I imagined myself as a master of double talk; tell them something plausible to deter them. For example, I remembered the fuel storage tanks I saw as we drove from the site of my capture and told them that they were our next attack plan. I reasoned that, if they believed me, they would go in a mad rush to camouflage and conceal the tanks. I hoped that flurry of activity would attract our pilots' attention and actually make the tanks a target. Each of the interrogators furiously made notes until one would leave the room for a few minutes to check the validity of my answers. When he returned he would talk to the others and the questioning would continue.

I was desperate for a drink of water and I could no longer feel my hands. I guessed it was now after midnight, a very long time since my capture and I had not tasted water since before I took off from Da Nang.

I humbly asked my interrogators for water. One of them went out the door, and to my surprise, a little old Vietnamese woman, perhaps fifty, walked into the room holding a tarnished old china cup filled with water. I guessed my positive response about the fuel storage tanks convinced them I was starting to cooperate.

Pigeye went behind my back and loosened the ratchet that tightened the handcuffs and removed them completely from my wrists. I had trouble maneuvering my arms to bring my hands to my front but finally managed to settle them in my lap. The woman held the water out to me and I anxiously reached for it with both hands but found I was unable to grasp the glass. My fingers would not do what my mind told them to do. I was so desperate for water that I managed to secure the glass between my wrists and tilt it up so that I could drink the warm water. It did not matter to me that the glass did not appear to be clean. If she had poured the water on the floor, I would have licked it up at this point. Never had water tasted so good to me.

When I looked up, the interrogators had left the room. I wondered where the old lady had gone as she had also disappeared. Alone, I decided to try to move around to see if my body would still function. I was able to walk if bent over from the waist but my arms, shoulders and hands still ached terribly.

Bug soon returned and informed me that my answers to their questions were not satisfactory. I had lied, he said, by swearing about the origin of my flight group. They knew that I had come from Cam Ranh Bay. He said they had captured many pilots and knew that was where my flight had originated. I would have to be punished for lying. I did not correct them knowing that the flight had actually originated in Da Nang. It was troubling to me that they somehow knew I was based at Cam Ranh Bay.

Pigeye and Buff were back in the room before I could

object and the torture immediately resumed. This time the leg stocks were forced down on my ankles even harder and blood squirted to the floor. As they inserted the iron bar behind my legs and tightened the straps to pull my head down, I wondered how long I would be able to endure the pain. Consciousness began to leave me and I thought of Steve. I was fortunate enough to attend his wedding in Durham, North Carolina in March of this year. I believed I would die soon and never get to see Steve and his lovely bride, Dale, again. I realized I was crying and as the tears flooded my face, I felt a peacefulness that I had not felt in a long time. I slipped into unconsciousness.

When I regained consciousness, the bar had been removed along with the ropes and straps. I was flat on my back with my hands still handcuffed behind me. I was lying in a pool of my own blood. There was a nasty, dirty piece of cloth in my mouth and the odor from it made me gag and choke. Pigeye and Buff were at my side and lifted me onto the low stool once again and removed the handcuffs.

I turned my head toward the door and could see that daylight was approaching. A shaft of light peeked through the crack between the doors. Being a perpetual optimist, I saw that delicate beam of light as a ray of hope. I paused and gave thanks to God for sparing my life through this night.

# Chapter 6

I looked down at my feet and they were grotesque, swollen beyond belief. They appeared to have been blown up like big balloons and had almost no feeling in them. As a youngster, I read the comics and Alley Oop was one of my favorites. His feet were always so unusual because they were out of proportion to the rest of his body. Here I was in a communist prison camp after one night of torture and I looked like Alley Oop and felt like I had been run over by a dinosaur.

I was not sure how many times I could take that much punishment and still maintain my sanity. Was it necessary for me to continue to refuse to answer their questions and suffer this inhumane treatment? They were putting an inordinate amount of pressure on me to break my spirit and to cause me to be cooperative with them.

I could not fail my country. I had to continue to resist their questions to the best of my ability. I would not give them any information gratuitously. They would have to extract it from me by force. I made up my mind that I would not, under any circumstances, give them or their Soviet allies any classified information about nuclear weapons or targets. I would let them torture me to death before I would divulge that category of information.

They were also seeking other military information of much lower precedence and sensitivity. I would try to avoid giving them any military information even though some of it was readily available in American media. At the same time, I knew that information they were after might not be available to them when they thought they needed it.

It was now fully daylight and I still had not been allowed to urinate. I asked, but they totally ignored me. The interrogators would be coming back soon with more questions. My bladder ached and I urgently needed to relieve myself to the point that I thought I might lose control at any second. I decided I would refuse to answer anything until I was allowed to go to the bathroom.

When the interrogators came into the room, I asked in a very positive but civil manner if I could use the bathroom. They instructed the guard to take me out of the room to relieve myself. We walked down the open passageway toward the room where I had been held a few hours before. We went across an open courtyard to a latrine located in the corner of the yard. I walked up a couple of steps and entered one of the most foul-smelling places I had ever been.

I could not use my hands because of the torture. I relieved myself by urinating in the pair of black shorts I wore. Thanks to the repeated blows to my lower back and kidneys, there was a considerable amount of blood in my urine.  When the guard decided he had given me sufficient time to relieve myself, he led me by the elbow back to the interrogation room which was Room Number 18.

The guard directed me to the lonesome looking stool that was still situated below the blue cloth covered table. I was relieved to see that the interrogators were not in the room as I squatted facing their empty chairs.  I guessed they had elected to take a break during my absence.

I decided to use the quiet time to clear my head and try to concentrate on the position I was in and how I should be conducting myself in the face of my enemies.  I reminded myself that as a member of the armed forces of the United States I was responsible for my conduct and actions while incarcerated after being captured by the enemy.  The fact that a state of war did not exist between my country and my captors did not relieve me of my responsibilities.

I knew that I must abide by the Code of Conduct for the American Fighting Man and the Uniform Code of Military Justice.  The Code of Conduct was created as a direct result of the Korean War when some members of the U.S. Armed Forces dishonored themselves and the United States by knowingly and willingly cooperating with the North Koreans.  It was one of the darkest pages in the history of our Armed Forces.

President Eisenhower appointed a special commission to study the problem and to recommend a code to govern the actions of America's Armed Forces.  As an officer of the U.S. Air Force, I had memorized the Code and found momentary strength by reciting it as I sat on the humbling stool awaiting more abuse.

*Article I: I am an American, fighting in the forces which guard my country and our way of life. I am prepared to give my life in their defense.*

*Article II: I will never surrender of my own free will. If in command, I will never surrender the members of my command while they still have the means to resist.*

*Article III: If I am captured I will continue to resist by all means available. I will make every effort to escape and to aid others to escape. I will accept neither parole nor special favors from the enemy.*

*Article IV: If I become a prisoner of war, I will keep faith with my fellow prisoners. I will give no information or take part in any action which might be harmful to my comrades. If I am senior, I will take command. If not, I will obey the lawful orders of those appointed over me and will back them up in every way.*

*Article V: When questioned, should I become a prisoner of war, I am required to give name, rank, service number, and date of birth. I will evade answering further questions to the utmost of my ability. I will make no oral or written statements disloyal to my country and its allies or harmful to their cause.*

*Article VI: I will never forget that I am an American, fighting for freedom, responsible for my actions and dedicated to the principles which made my country free. I will trust in my God and in the United States of America.*

I knew that the Uniform Code of Military Justice was forceful and supported by rule of law that would stand up in a military court while the Code of Conduct was more of a guideline for rules of conduct. But to me, one was the same as the other where my personal conduct was concerned.

My mental recitations were interrupted when the horrible group of three marched back through the double doors. The questions were a continuation from last night. They wanted military information and they wanted it now.

I decided to deceive them and concoct a cover story that would stop the torture. I had to keep in mind that Jim Jefferson might be under interrogation somewhere if he was still alive. I did not want to say anything that would incriminate him.

Sometime during the questioning, they brought in three of their pilots. They asked questions concerning formations and tactics. I never gave a definitive answer to any of the questions. I evasively responded that sometimes we did things one way and sometimes a totally different way.

The pilots were interested in specific information on the Sidewinder missile and the recently introduced Electronic Counter Measures pod. I managed to avoid any questions about the missile and the pod by explaining that I was not a technical officer but rather a pilot. Much to my surprise and relief, the pilots did not seem interested in the performance aspects of the F-4 aircraft. They did not ask any questions about the airplane. Perhaps they had gleaned all the information they wanted from pilots who were captured before me.

Interrogation was a painfully slow process. Generally, all three of the interrogators would arrive to start the session, then one would leave and return later to talk with the other two. They compared notes and talked in a normal tone of voice. As they talked, I listened just as intently as possible, hoping to make them think I understood some of what they were saying. Actually, I did not understand anything. After a discussion period, a different one would leave the room.

Their understanding of English was fair at best and I tried to exploit their weakness by pretending not to understand them or by giving a totally ambiguous answer that had nothing to do with the question. They grew frustrated and threatened to punish me many times.

I was determined not to reveal to them that I was the Assistant Deputy Commander for Operations of the 12th Tactical Fighter Wing at Cam Ranh Bay. Cam Ranh Air Base was one of the most active bases in the southern part of Vietnam. Our 12th Tactical Fighter Wing was the parent organization. With its affiliated groups, more than ten thousand personnel operated our aircraft around the clock nonstop. Since Travis McNeil and I shared the operational duties day and night, we scheduled ourselves to fly at least every other day. It was important for us to lead the missions and to understand the problems of the air crews.

I arrived at Cam Ranh in late November of 1966 and began to fly combat missions in early December. As a Colonel, I was scheduled for a one year tour of duty. My first missions were as a wing man and then as an element leader. After learning the ropes, I began to lead missions in and near the Demilitarized Zone (DMZ) at the 17th parallel and in Laos.

Toward the end of 1966, the Viet Cong began rocket attacks on U.S. air bases in South Vietnam. At first, the attacks were more of a harassing action than anything else. But, with the passage of time, it became evident that the VC wanted to inflict severe damage on at least one American air base. They hoped to repeat their previous successful performance when, in November of 1964, they carried out a well-planned attack on Bien Hoa airbase with 81 mm mortars. The attack destroyed five B-57 aircraft and damaged fifteen more. Four Americans were killed and seventy-two were wounded. But the tide of the war was not favoring the VC by early 1967. Their infrastructure was crumbling and they needed a psychological victory.

# Chapter 7

The interrogations dragged through the next twenty-four hours requiring that I repeat the answers to the same questions over and over. They were determined to trip me up and cause me to alter my responses. I knew when that happened it would give them an excuse to resume the torture.

I slowly developed a credible story of being stationed at MacDill Air Force Base in Tampa, Florida. I carefully wove a tale that I thought I could make them believe. I was a training officer for air crews coming to Vietnam. I had to train them to fly the F-4 and to use all of its weapons.

I was sent to Vietnam to evaluate our training program and to gather information first-hand because of some reported problems. I was to fly combat missions with the crews so that I could understand their problems and needs. On my first mission I was shot down and captured. Due to the nature of my job, I did not know anything about war plans or weapons and I was not in a decision making position.

They appeared to be buying my story. They continued to interrogate me but eased off on the torture as they intermittently returned to gain clarity or ask me for more details about my statements.

Even during intense periods of torture, I could not stop thinking about Jim Jefferson. I kept reviewing my knowledge of events as I remembered them. I knew that I had advised him to eject although our communication was difficult and in crisis. I remembered hearing the racket when his canopy released. I had to presume that his ejection was successful since I did not have a visual confirmation. I was too preoccupied with trying to control the aircraft that was spinning and tumbling to be able to focus.

I did see Jim's name tag and helmet in the possession of my captors so I knew they either captured him or took them from his body. I guessed that it was most likely he ejected but knew it was also possible that he could have crashed with the airplane. I hoped he was alive and here at the Hanoi Hilton somewhere.

Bug kept trying to interrogate me about my family. I refused to tell him anything until I got some information about Jim. I asked Bug where he was and if he was okay. He responded with a curious question with hopes of tripping me up. He asked, "Did you know his father?" I told him I did not and that I met Jim for the first time at noon on the day we were shot down. That was one of the only truths they would get from me and it fit perfectly with my story that I was on my first mission.

Jim was a handsome young man and a 1964 graduate

of the Air Force Academy. He had flown several missions to North Vietnam and gone "downtown" (the term we used to describe bombing the city of Hanoi) a number of times. I had flown numerous bombing missions over North Vietnam, but since this was to be my first trip downtown, his experience was especially helpful as we prepared our maps and flight cards. He exuded great confidence as he led me through the process.

After our formal briefings with the rest of the flight crew, we spent some time together just talking about the mission and how we intended to support those who would be taking an external gun pod along for the first time. The external gun pod that looked sort of like a torpedo encasement was attached to the belly of the F-4 and added machine gun capability to aid in air-to-air or other confrontations that needed fire support during bombing runs. This was an historic event and we were both fired up about it. It would be even more exciting if our flight could surprise the MIG pilots and shoot them down using the new pods.

Surprise is one of the most important principles of war and a primary consideration during the planning of our bombing missions. Our best chance to surprise the North Vietnamese was the first thing in the morning before the sun was fully up, when the cover of darkness could be our friend. At the same time we needed visibility to be able to ascertain and confirm our targets so we scheduled our earliest strikes between 7:30 and 9:30 each morning.

Once the morning missions were complete, the pilots would return to their bases to rearm and refuel for a second mission that we would normally target for between 2:00 and 4:00 in the afternoon. If anyone had to bail out on the second mission, there would still be enough daylight left to get the rescue forces in and try to recover those who had crashed or bailed out. If our people were on the ground as the sun was setting, the darkness would suddenly become our most dreaded foe. These time constraints often made the element of surprise nothing more than a pipe dream.

Air raid sirens blasted in the midst of the interrogation. Bug, the interrogators and the guards ran from the room leaving me on the stool with my hands still cuffed behind me. The sound of our bombs exploding in the distance brought me joy at a time when I did not think it was possible for me to feel any kind of positive emotion. I found myself wishing that the bombs would hit closer and perhaps even take out some of this terrible place, but I knew that would be an unrealistic hope without killing or injuring prisoners. I sure did enjoy seeing the fear and panic in the faces and reactions of my enemies, though.

I discovered that I was not frightened even when the bombs exploded near the prison walls. If I was going to die here, I would rather it be from our bombs than by the hands of my enemies. I wanted the bombing to continue non-stop. It gave me hope that my country was continuing to force the North Vietnamese to negotiate so we could go home.

I made a private attempt at humor imagining that I was enjoying a two-night stay at the Hanoi Hilton with the third night free, "free of torture that is." Even though bombs exploded near the prison, none were close enough for bomb fragments to land within the walls.

I feared for the air crews and said a prayer for them. I knew the flack that they would be getting and expected there was an air war taking place above me. I just hoped our guys were winning and no more prisoners would be taken.

I was disappointed when the bombing ended and my enemies returned. They attempted to conceal the fear among them, but their woeful facial expressions revealed their true cowardice. Even knowing that they would be offended and likely punish me, I could not help but show them that I was elated that our bombers were striking.

I could see that my efforts succeeded when they proceeded to tell me many "U.S. air pirates" had been shot down. I knew that during our many raids we seldom lost aircraft so it was clear to me they were propagandizing to me just as they would be doing in their news releases to their people and the world.

A guard brought in a bowl of clear liquid soup, some rice and a small banana. I tried to drink the soup, but I spilled most of it. I could not hold a spoon so I bent over and drank the soup much like a dog or cat would lap it up. I put my face in the rice bowl and ate as much as I could.

69

The guard smirked when I motioned that I could not peel the banana and I had no intention of asking him to peel it for me.

I was hungry and my stomach ached, but food was not appealing to me in my current condition and circumstance. My instinct for survival told me I had to eat regardless how degrading it felt or how disgusting the nourishment seemed that was presented to me. I just would not allow myself to dwell on the thought of food. It was too painful.

I needed water more than I needed food. They would not give it to me unless I begged for it and that was brutal. I also needed medical attention now for the lacerations on my ankles and legs. I no longer had any feeling in my feet. When I looked down at my feet, they were covered with mosquitoes and flies. I had neither shoes nor sandals. My feet were so swollen that I could not have worn them anyway.

On Sunday morning, my second full day in captivity, our airplanes were overhead again on a mission to bomb targets somewhere in the vicinity of Hanoi. The flak guns seemed to be ringed around the prison camp and I was awed by the amount of anti-aircraft firing that took place. I could distinguish the whoosh of SAMs as they lifted off to intercept the attacking aircraft. Too soon the all clear siren blared. Each raid brought hope. Each departure left disappointment and depression.

The afternoon raid was far more intense and thankfully

prolonged. I could visualize our special F-4's in a dog fight with the MIGs. I hoped that our pilots had a lot of success when I was shot down and I desperately wished that they were back today to deliver the coup de grace to the Vietnamese Air Force.

I wanted to believe that our guys were making the enemy pay for shooting my airplane out of the sky. I prayed that our missions were whittling away at their limited supply of pilots. At the same time, I knew that if some of their planes were shot down with the gun pod, I would be under extreme pressure to describe the pod.

My wandering mind returned to January when our forces shot down seven MIGs in what was pegged as "Operation BoLo." I wanted Boots and his F-4 pilots to carve a niche for themselves, just as our forces had done in that special deception operation. I knew the communists were still chafing about those losses.

Again the all clear sounded and my interrogators promptly returned. I had not actually slept since I left Da Nang and I felt like I was having an out of body experience. Relentlessly, they continued with their questions. Did the American people support the war? Was the United States going to invade North Vietnam? How many troops would the United States send to South Vietnam? What were the next important targets to be bombed? Would the U.S. bomb Hanoi with B-52s? I pleaded ignorance or responded with evasive answers to their questions.

They wanted to know how much knowledge I had about the National Liberation Front (NLF) that was founded in 1960 to build up the North's insurgency in the South. My memory was that it was a combination of regular army and cadres of organized South Vietnamese peasants. These people, referred to as the Viet Cong, would include many former Viet Minh who had settled in the North after the 1954 Geneva Accords divided Vietnam at the 17th Parallel with Ho Chi Minh in the north and the Diem government and French Union forces in the south. Nearly 900,000 citizens from the north migrated south as a result of the Accords while about 52,000, mostly Viet Minh and their families migrated north.

The North propagandized that the NLF was indigenous to the south, created and occupied by dissident South Vietnamese citizens who were unhappy that the government declined to hold national elections. The United States and the South Vietnamese governments claimed that the NLF was a tool created by the North to infiltrate and organize as their partners against the South Vietnamese government and their American allies.

My interrogators tried to brain wash me into believing that North Vietnam had never done anything to organize, equip, train, direct or finance the National Liberation Front in South Vietnam. I was not sympathetic to their story and their efforts to make me feel remorse for my role supporting the South fell on deaf ears. At the same time, I thought it would be best not to try to argue the politics of the war and events leading to it and decided to feign ignorance rather than let them know I was aware of the true history. I knew antagonizing them unnecessarily could get me killed.

The team of interrogators continued to hammer me with questions, twisting my answers to fit their desired responses in an effort to confuse me. The sessions went on hour after hour. They were determined to use my fatigue, injuries, hunger and thirst to wear me down. Occasionally, they would leave for several hours, warning me that if I slept or attempted to leave my little stool they would kill me. I assumed that they were also interrogating other pilots somewhere in the prison. Every few minutes, a guard would open the door to check on me.

My body got some seriously needed rest during these periods of their absence and I would regain some strength. I remained awake by feverishly working my mind, partly out of fear from their threat but mostly because I had to remember what I had told them as I wove fictitious responses. I could not let them punch holes in my cover story.

The short stool was most uncomfortable. All of my weight seemed to rest only on my buttocks. I squirmed and turned first on one cheek and then the other. Fatigue and lack of sleep were beginning to take their toll and my mind was not functioning well.

Somehow I managed to stay awake throughout the

night. My whole body ached. I was thirsty, hungry and very sleepy.

I began to think about Jim Jefferson. Was he okay? Had he been captured and brought into prison? If he were here, how was he handling the interrogation? Would our stories match? I had no reason to think that he would give in to their questions, but if he were seriously injured or delirious, he might reveal some information that could help the Vietnamese interrogators piece together a picture of what happened on our mission.

When not being questioned by the Vietnamese, my thoughts always turned to my family. I wondered if Hazel would remain in Winston-Salem when she learned that I was shot down. But, then I realized that of course she would need to be there to help provide care for her mother who was ailing from cancer. At the same time she would need her mother's support while she waited to learn my fate.

I hoped Steve would not allow my capture to interrupt or negatively affect his schooling at Duke where he was now twenty-one and in his junior year. Only six weeks ago, Steve married Dale Watson, the daughter of a career Navy officer. Dale was a graduate of Duke and was doing post-graduate work at Emory University. Steve and Dale were much alike; quiet, sensitive, studious, patriotic and filled with dreams of a golden future.

Tony, now eleven, was a free spirit if ever there was one. If we had allowed him, he would have been a school dropout in the third grade. Tony was born during my assignment to Germany. School was not his bag. He viewed it as totally unnecessary since it interfered with his "freedom". Ruth Stanley, our neighbor and a school teacher while we were in Falls Church, Virginia, helped to improve Tony's study skills and that resulted in a better attitude toward school.

My mother in Knoxville, now widowed, was sixty-five years old and would be devastated by the news of my missing-in-action status. She had already lost her other son on Omaha Beach in June of 1944. Her heart had to be heavy. Fortunately, my younger sister lived nearby and would help to comfort her while I languished in a North Vietnamese prison.

My greatest concern for my family was for them to know that I survived the bailout and was in relatively good physical condition. However, the possibility of hearing that from me seemed to be growing more remote each time I confronted the Vietnamese interrogators.

I was determined to maintain my sanity. I learned in survival training to put myself into sort of a self-induced trance, a method to retreat into my mind when the physical world became too harsh. I would recant pleasant memories, paying close attention to details as a distraction from current reality. I needed to stay awake so I made a conscious effort to take myself back to Knoxville, Hazel and my early days in the Air Force.

# Chapter 8

I was seventeen years old when the Ketner family moved into their dry cleaning plant that also served as their home on Main Street in East Knoxville. I was immediately attracted to their lovely daughter. There were other young men who also noticed this charming girl, including my older brother, Ralph. Hazel worked in her parents' dry cleaning plant and she also worked part time as a cashier in a food chain store. She appeared to be about sixteen years old, but I later learned that she was only fourteen.

She was radiant and charming. I was determined to learn all that I could about her, including when and where she attended school, where she spent her time and what interested her. I was excited to learn that she was a freshman at Knoxville High School where I also attended. It was no coincidence when soon after, I happened to be walking to school on her street and on her schedule and managed to find an excuse to walk along beside her.

I walked to school with her every chance I got after that first meeting. She must have had a little interest in me as well since she never refused when I offered to meet to walk along with her. Since I worked after school, I never got to see her in the afternoons.

I finally got up the courage to ask her for a date and invited her to accompany me to our school's football game on a Friday night. I was able to get off of work when our team played at home. After the game, we walked to the Krispy Kreme donut shop and bought a dozen fresh warm donuts for sixty cents. Donuts in hand, we went to the grocery store down the street and bought a quart of cold milk for ten cents. We went to her house and ate all of the donuts and shared the milk. At our age, who was worried about calories? After that first date, there was never any question in my mind that Hazel and I would become a couple.

The two of us were a lot alike. We took our responsibilities to our families and jobs very seriously. We were children during the depression years and our parents struggled to get by day to day like most other people during those difficult times. My grandparents were farmers and were more prepared than most to survive the hard times. We had food on our table when many others went hungry.

I was eighteen when the Japanese bombed Pearl Harbor on December 7, 1941. Our country had to quickly mobilize to fight a war on two fronts, against an aggressive Japan in the Pacific and the Germans in Europe. Ammunition plants, aircraft plants and automotive plants throughout America began operating twenty-four hours a day.

We were fighting enemies who had been planning and

preparing for war for many years while our nation hoped to remain isolated from the conflict. For the first several months of 1942, our nation was struggling for its life. Everyone had to sacrifice to meet the needs of the country. Rationing gas, tires, sugar and other items became a way of life. Thousands of young men and women volunteered for service. Nearly every home in our neighborhood had one or two family members in service. Unlike other wars, our country was attacked and all of us young men were determined to step up to the challenge.

Hazel's brother, Douglas, had joined the Marine Corps in the summer of 1941. He finished boot camp just before the Japanese attack. His division, the 1st Marine Division, was hurriedly sent to Guadalcanal Island in the southwest Pacific Ocean. My brother, Ralph, was drafted into the Army in the summer of 1942. I did not understand all of the reasons why the United States was attacked by Japan and why we were being drawn into war in Europe. However, like most of my friends, I felt a strong obligation to serve my country even though my potential role or contribution was unclear to me. I wanted to enlist in the Army Air Corps. In spite of my parents' strong objections, I went to the recruiting office and signed up "for the duration plus six months."

I promised Hazel that I would stay in touch with her and I asked for a small picture that I could keep in my wallet. I was very much in love with her. Our goodbyes were tearful and emotional as the day for my induction arrived.

# Chapter 9

My first stop was at Camp Forrest in Tullahoma, Tennessee where I was officially welcomed into the Army Air Corps on October 29, 1942. After the swearing in ceremony, we stood in line to get our uniforms then on to another line for shots. It was a little traumatic to get shots in both shoulders at once. A few of the inductees fainted dead away from fear of needles. I was not wild about the experience but managed to bare my shoulders and stand erect to endure the process.

I went from Camp Forrest to the Classification Center at Fort Oglethorpe in Georgia. It felt like someone must have gotten confused because I found myself in another line for shots before being directed to collect additional uniforms. Then on to processing where the desk clerk informed me that since I participated in Reserve Officer Training at Knoxville High School, I would be exempt from normally required basic training.

My first real assignment took me to a combat crew training base known as Page Army Air Field in Fort Myers, Florida. When our load of recruits stepped off of the bus at about ten in the evening, a "man-eating" First Sergeant greeted us. I had wrongly assumed that bypassing basic training had exempted me from the drill sergeant abuses I had heard so much about from other soldiers. He hammered us with a string of four-letter words to drive home the point that we now belonged to him and failing to obey his every command would unleash the wrath of God. Then, with feigned humility and oozing with sarcasm, he instructed us to address him as "First Sergeant" instead of "God".

He marched us to supply where we added bedding to our load of clothing and boots, then on to get our housing assignments. I should not have been surprised to learn that our housing consisted of giant "green tents lined with folding canvas cots. The First Sergeant administered a twenty minute block of instruction on how to properly make up a military bed before sending us off to our tent assignments.

It was now approaching midnight and the single dangling light bulb in the center of our tent was turned off. We stumbled around with all of our gear until someone found the light and flipped it on. A gruff sounding soldier in the tent must have had a bad day and screamed at us to "TURN THE LIGHT OFF!" There was a sudden muzzle flash and explosion as that angry soldier shot the light out. We all managed to stealthily find and make our cots in the dark. We were so quiet you would not have known anyone was in the tent much less making beds and stowing gear.

Everything seemed to happen at warp speed after that

Bill Norris

intimidating first night on the post. I was assigned to a squadron as a mechanic on a Martin B-26 airplane. As an on-the-job trainee I pulled my share of kitchen police and other mundane details so much so that I did not have time to be homesick, although I thought of Hazel constantly. She sent me inspirational letters that followed me all through my whirlwind indoctrination into military life and helped to keep me grounded and focused.

One of the two sergeants I reported to allowed me to fly as a passenger on a short flight. It was my first flight and I was hooked as I looked out over South Florida and the Everglades. I was disappointed when we landed at the 36th Street Airport in Miami. I wanted more.

On December 12, 1942, the Combat Crew Training Wing moved by convoy from Fort Myers to Avon Park, Florida. I was impressed by the extent of military organization as we loaded gear and troops onto the trucks and accomplished the entire move in one day.

At Avon Park we lived in temporary wooden huts arranged around a common latrine. The huts were designed so the lower sections were wood and the upper third were screened sidewalls that opened up to allow light and fresh air in. Each hut had two oil fired stoves and several overhead lights and would accommodate thirty beds. Compared to Page Field, this was the Ritz.

In January of 1943, I was promoted to corporal and my pay scale went up to $66 per month. I applied for a three-day pass that worked out to be five days including the

82

weekend so I boarded a bus for Knoxville anxious to see Hazel and my family.

I was excited to see my brother for the last time before his infantry division moved from Camp Atterbury, Indiana to England. He confided in me that he had managed to get into training to become a medic since he did not want to kill people. It was just not in his nature. He wanted to help those who had been wounded in battle and liked the idea of carrying medical supplies instead of a rifle. After my talk with him, I sincerely believed that, if he lived through the war, he would serve in the ministry or in a humanitarian organization.

My weekend at home passed too quickly. When I returned to Avon Park, a group of aircrews arrived in our squadron who had completed combat tours in the Aleutian Chain in Alaska. Instead of being promoted as officers, they were staff sergeants. At the beginning of the war, the Army Air Corps lacked the funds to promote all pilots, navigators and bombardiers to commissioned officers.

These staff sergeants had flown twenty-five missions against the Japanese forces in the Chain. In an effort to compensate them, the Air Corps promoted some of them to the grade of Flight Officer, a rank below Second Lieutenant. Those who were not promoted were allowed to apply to go to flight training. The cadets who successfully completed their training would be commissioned as Second Lieutenants.

When the opportunity to go to flight training was

posted, it was open not just to those staff sergeants, so I added my name. I was sent to Hendricks Army Air Field which was about ten miles from Avon Park. I passed the battery of mental and physical exams and was accepted to flying school.

I was pleasantly surprised to learn that I would be allowed to go home on furlough before reporting for training. The military had once again allowed me unexpected time to solidify my relationship with my precious Hazel. However, it was short lived since a telegraph messenger arrived with an urgent order for me to immediately return to base for a new assignment.

I was going to Keesler Field in Biloxi, Mississippi. I was surprised, and somewhat disappointed, to learn that applying for flight school would require me to take a step backwards and complete basic training which I had managed to avoid up to now.

I proudly completed six weeks of vigorous physical and mental basic in stifling heat and humidity. The mean First Sergeant at Avon Park turned out to be a teddy bear compared to the drill instructors in Biloxi. Upon graduation from basic, I was loaded along with two hundred other cadets off to the State Teachers College in Eau Claire, Wisconsin. During the next four months, we underwent strenuous preflight training.

Upon completion of the training in early December of 1943, our class was sent by train to Santa Ana, California. It took seven days to make the trip. Our train did not have a very high priority and we spent several hours on sidings waiting for other higher priority trains to pass us. We arrived in the Los Angeles area about the same time as what seemed like the monsoon season. It rained incessantly.

The personnel at the processing center formed us into squadrons of two-hundred and twenty-five men each. Then on to another series of mental, physical and psychological tests to determine which of us would train as pilots, navigators or bombardiers.

The military portion of our training was long and strenuous. I felt like I was back in basic training. The Army Air Corps needed soldiers who could withstand unusual levels of stress and duress. It certainly tested our fortitude. Surprisingly, only a few people were eliminated.

Our military and academic instructors were all eager young officers. The academic officers were available to work with us at night if we felt we needed them. Like basic training, we were restricted to the base for the first six weeks to insure we dedicated sufficient time to our physical training and studies.

The preflight training lasted three months, then on to primary flight training which would take place either in California or Arizona. I was selected to go to the Ryan School of Aeronautics at Hemet, California. The school was staffed by civilians and was owned and operated by the Ryan Aircraft Company. The overall Commander of the school was an Army Air Corps Major. He had a staff of military check pilots who were there to ensure that the training met military standards.

We were like kids with new toys the first time we marched to the flight line and saw the PT-22 airplanes and met our instructors. Each instructor had four students. Our academic instructors were civilians as were our flight line crews. Many of the flight line personnel were women, some very pretty. But we could not have any personal or social contact with them whether on or off base.

Many of the cadets were not as fortunate as I was to have a sweetheart back home. I could not help but feel compassion for some of the guys as I watched and listened to them pining over the women who were flirtatious and appeared to be unattached. I guessed that there were probably some secret liaisons going on.

Unlike the way we were treated during our training up to now, our military instructors treated us honorably, much like you would expect at the services academies. We were finally finished with those tough sergeants. I was now addressed as Mr. Gaddis and it felt good.

The Primary Flying Training Program was designed to provide students up to eight hours of dual instruction before allowing us to solo. I soloed after seven hours and gladly surrendered to my ceremonial toss into the swimming pool. That achievement confirmed for me that I had made the right choice to pursue pilot training.

Our class finished seventy hours of flying in two and a half months and we were ready to move into the basic phase of training. Our next flight school was at Cal-Aero Flying Academy in Ontario, California, about fifty miles from Hemet. Cal-Aero was the only basic flying school in the western states having civilian flight instructors.

Our living accommodations were a considerable upgrade from anything I had seen in my time in the Army Air Corps up to now. The buildings were single story stucco structures that accommodated two cadets in each spacious room. Instead of a large group latrine, we shared a bathroom with two cadets in the adjacent room. Our training commitment in Ontario was for another six-week period of confinement to base.

The BT-13 airplane was larger and more powerful than the PT-22's we flew at Hemet. They were much faster and had closed cockpits and radios. The landing gear was fixed, not retractable. The academics required to support the higher class of airplane were extremely technical and far more difficult.

About mid-point through our training, I was not paying close enough attention to my health and became dehydrated. Our superiors told us to take salt tablets that were readily available in our mess hall but I was not as diligent as I should have been. I began to have severe stomach cramps. About the same time, I received word from my mother that my brother, Ralph, was killed on June 12, 1944 during the D-Day invasion of Europe.

The news was devastating and further weakened my already poor physical condition. The medics cancelled my flying status and put me in a clinic. A few days later, after showing no marked improvement in my condition, I thought of asking to go home to be allowed time to recuperate and pay proper respects to Ralph. I did not want to fall behind and get held back and separated from the close associations I had made with my classmates, so I made the heart rending decision not to go home to be with my parents. I knew it would be hard on them, but my country was still at war and I was determined to follow through with my commitments.

With the proper medications and improved attention to my health and hydration, I was soon ready to return to flight ready status. My flight instructor was a compassionate man and he worked me into the flying schedule so that I could catch up on what I had missed during my absence. My roommates were also supportive and helpful as I worked my way through the mental stress of losing my brother.

Our class was referred to as the lower class for the first six weeks. When the class ahead of us moved on to advanced training at another base, we became the upper class for the final six weeks of our training. This proved to be a pivotal point in my training and development as a pilot since our class was divided into two categories. I would either further train to become a pilot for single engine fighters and trainers or be assigned to train to fly multi-engine, bomber, transport and rescue airplanes.

Some of the larger and taller men who wanted to fly fighters were disappointed when their multi-engine assignments were posted. I was relieved to make the list for fighter training and was sent to Williams Army Air Field in Chandler, Arizona, about fifteen miles southeast of Phoenix. When we arrived in Phoenix at midnight, the temperature was still a hundred degrees.

Our housing was traditional two-story Army style wooden buildings. They were equipped with evaporative coolers which were effective since the humidity was typically only four to five percent. The normal average rainfall during July, August and September was almost zero.

The buildings for our academic studies were nearby, but the flight line was at least half of a mile away. In grueling heat, we marched daily as squadrons of forty-five cadets to and from our academic training and the flight line. To remain presentable and pass inspections, we had to launder one of our two lightweight flight suits to replace the one we soiled with sweat every day. The heat required us to take two daily salt tablets with lots of water to keep us hydrated.

Our introduction to this phase of training began with indoctrination lectures which defined the progression our lives as student pilots would take for the next six weeks, then on to meet our flight instructors. As we approached the flight line, the stifling heat did not seem as noticeable once I caught sight of the first Air Corps fighter airplane I had seen. It was an RP-322, a P-38 Lightning without super-charged engines. It was beautiful and I could hardly keep my eyes straight ahead while in formation. But then, like taking candy away from a baby, our flight instructors informed us that we would not be flying that airplane. Apparently, several cadets had been killed while flying it.

Further down the flight line our instructors introduced us to our training airplane, the AT-6 made by North American Aircraft Company. It was slightly larger and had a more powerful engine than the BT-13 we flew in Ontario. They told us that it had one bad characteristic called ground looping. During landing it had a tendency to veer off the runway on the last part of the landing roll. You did not know whether it was going to skew left or right which could be extra tricky. There was no way to anticipate it so recovery was totally dependent on instantaneous pilot reaction times. Most pilots could not react fast enough and the airplane would leave the runway and spin around in the dirt.

According to our instructors, there were two types of AT-6 pilots, those who had already ground looped and those who were waiting to ground loop. I joined the club after I graduated from flying school. I had flown a gunnery mission at Ajo, Arizona, and I ground looped on landing. I was amazed how quickly it happened. Somehow, I managed not to damage the airplane. It certainly made a believer out of me as I sent rabbits scrambling that were playing in the scrub nearby.

# Chapter 10

The sudden awareness of pain in every part of my body that wasn't numb brought me back to my current reality. I had no idea whether I had been immersed in my memories for minutes or hours. With a foggy stare, I looked around the room and saw that I was still alone. They were undoubtedly checking out my story with information gathered from other prisoners.

I was relieved to see that it would soon be daylight, but chagrined with the realization that it would not be long before they began interrogating me again. So far, I had done a good job of protecting the military information that I held. As the rays of sun peeked through the edges of the covered windows and cracks in the door frame, the memory world that occupied my brain while I was sitting in darkness began to clear. I became more alert to my surroundings and aware of what seemed to be a lot of activity by people in the courtyard. I began to desperately wish for some kind of contact with fellow Americans.

My thoughts were abruptly interrupted as the door to the interrogation room slammed open and my interrogators marched single file to their positions behind the blue cloth covered table. Two of the interrogators sat facing me and instantly tore into their incessant questioning. They began by asking the same questions as before, but with more intensity and impatience.

They then shifted their focus to U.S. plans. They demanded that I tell them about the overall war plan which they appeared to be convinced that I knew. Then they insisted I tell them which targets would be bombed today. I repeatedly responded that I was not a war planner and that I really did not know anything about target priorities and locations.

During the late morning hours, the guards brought in some clear broth and rice. Although I was very hungry, I spilled most of the soup as I tried to drink it. My hands were practically useless. I could not grasp the small aluminum spoon. The guard moved in and out of the room several times as I tried to eat. He was trying to see if I was faking it or if I really had been injured during the torture session.

Once I managed to finish eating, the guard took me outside to a foul smelling latrine. I managed to do my business, but since I did not have the use of my hands, it was much as a dog would accomplish these trivial survival tasks.

As I walked back across the prison yard, I sensed that it was ghostly quiet and that there was not a soul in sight. I would later learn that this quiet hour was a daily routine. Due to the extremely hot and humid weather, the Vietnamese spent two or three hours resting after the midday meal. However, there was no rest for me.

The moment I was back on the midget stool that was fast becoming my body's number one enemy, the interrogators were coming back at me harder than ever. They wanted information and any effort I made to stall infuriated them. I continued to avoid answering questions by saying that I did not know the answer. I also reverted to my prior tactic of pretending that I did not understand what they were asking. Since their English was only fair at best, I felt it would seem reasonable for me to be confused.

Between each series of questions, I concentrated as hard as I could to try to recall specifics of survival training that would apply to my situation. In 1952 I attended a survival course at Stead Air Force Base in Nevada. Many of our instructors had been prisoners during World War II. They taught us how to avoid answering questions and how to frustrate the interrogators. Other instructors had been interrogators and they described the techniques of forcibly extracting information from prisoners.

This round of questioning had not been underway very long before the air raid siren blasted and the interrogators scurried from the room. The nearby flak guns roared as they fired at our pilots. Occasionally, I could hear the SAMs as they lifted off attempting to intercept our fighters.

I could tell that the bombing target was somewhere in the downtown area. I could feel the percussion in my eardrums as the bombs found their targets. The blue curtains on the door flapped about and the doors rattled. I could not see outside the room but my spirits soared high with our pilots as they bombed the targets.

Sadly, the air raid only lasted ten to twelve minutes. I sorely yearned for it to continue until there was no more Pigeye, no more Buff, no more Bug and no more North Vietnam.

Sometime during the afternoon Bug returned to reason with me. He was frustrated with me and my attitude. It was obvious that he and the other interrogators were under great pressure to get information from the first Air Force Colonel captured in North Vietnam. Other colonels had been shot down but they apparently did not survive.

Bug tried to appeal to my conscience by describing in great detail how the U.S. was committing aggression against a small and innocent nation. I was defiant in letting him know through my words and expressions that his garbage was not getting through.

Finally, in desperation, he wanted to strike a bargain with me. He informed me that, if I would cooperate and answer his questions, I would live better and receive medical attention, be given clothes and, finally, I would be able to communicate with my family.

Even under my desperate circumstances, I managed an indignant posture and response. I was determined that I would not cooperate with them even if I never had the chance to write to my family. I knew that cooperating would allow them to dominate me, my actions and my credibility to my fellow prisoners in the camp. Even unto death, I vowed that would never happen.

Bug asked me if I thought I would ever go home. I responded emphatically that I would go home, and that I would go home with honor. Bug suggested that I could appeal to the President and/or Congress to stop the war and withdraw U.S. troops from South Vietnam. I could write a letter and apologize to the North Vietnamese people for my actions and the actions of my country or I could request amnesty from the North Vietnamese and possibly be released early to return home. Despite all of my physical and emotional distress, I was not about to cave in and commit treason for that little Communist bastard.

It grieved me to know that the position I had taken would deny me the opportunity to let my family know that I was alive and it played havoc with my emotions. My captors knew that was the one most important thing in life to me, the ace they intended to play to break me. But I knew Hazel would be devastated if she learned that I had broken, especially if she had been used as the pawn. I knew my honor and her respect for me rode in the balance of what I did or did not do this day.

I had always believed that adversity tends to bring out the best qualities in us whether it is during a time of war or in peace. Some intangible quality seems to rise up in us and give us strength and courage. Nevertheless, sometimes we fail to meet our own expectations. Why this happens, perhaps we will never know.

By late afternoon, it became apparent to me that I had provoked the Vietnamese into torturing me again. The interrogators talked quietly among themselves and periodically one or two would leave the room. Eventually, Bug came in to inform me that I was to be punished again because I would not abide by camp regulations. His left eye was rotating slowly and he had a sneer on his face.

Pigeye and Buff rattled and banged into the room with their torture equipment. I tried to shrink into myself at the dread of having to go through this again. This time, they roughly shoved me from the stool and ordered me to sit on the floor with my back against the wall. They stretched my legs out straight in front of me.

Pigeye and Buff put the iron stocks on my legs by placing their feet on my shins and forcing my legs down. The blood started to flow again and it was excruciatingly painful. They inserted the iron bar through the eyelets so that the weight of the bar rested on my legs. The bar felt like it weighed a ton, although it probably only weighed about twenty-five pounds.

I sat shackled for the next four or five hours while the interrogators asked questions about the gun pods that we carried on two of the aircraft in our flight. The pain in my feet and ankles was horrible. The North Vietnamese had evidently learned that 7th Air Force Headquarters in

Saigon had issued a press release about our mission. Armed with the new information, my interrogators were coming at me hard for more information on the gun pods. I had to assume that our pilots had shot down some of their airplanes on the Saturday afternoon mission. Otherwise, why would they be so interested in our new weapon?

It excited me to think that maybe we got some of them on the day they took me prisoner. It filled me with renewed resolve to beat them at their interrogation game no matter how much pain I had to endure. All the while it filled me with renewed fear of the torture I would have to tolerate thanks to the public announcements by my flight commanders.

By the time the interrogation was over, my ankles were stuck to the leg stocks with blood. My buttocks were raw and bleeding and the black underpants were stuck to me. I ached all over. I was desperate for rest and sleep. I wondered how long I could continue to resist the interrogators.

Sometime after midnight, Pigeye and Buff roughly removed the leg stocks seeming to enjoy the added pain it caused me. I stared at my swollen feet and bloody ankles and wondered if I would ever recover from this ordeal. I took pride in knowing that my resolve had not been broken and I had managed, at a price, to resist providing any worthwhile information to the interrogators about the gun pod.

The camp was quiet. It was late night and I found myself hoping that the darkness would be my friend. Perhaps I had outlasted my interrogators and they would succumb to their own need for rest. The silence was broken by the chimes from the clock that I had seen outside of the prison. It was not only an ironically comforting sound, it was my only means of tracking time. It was now 2:00 AM. Maybe even I could get some sleep.

That was not to happen. Much to my surprise, Pigeye came into the room and motioned for me to follow him. He led me through a couple of dark passageways and stopped next to a door with louvered shutters along the bottom. He directed me to enter the room that I quickly observed was no more than seven feet long by seven feet wide. It had a single electric light bulb hanging from the starkly barren ceiling. The room was completely bare. A guard brought a bowl of warm rice broth and I slurped as much as I could before I fell asleep.

Although severely fatigued, I slipped into a twilight state between dreams and memories and in my mind became the sane and stable person I was before all of this insanity began.

# Chapter 11

My instructor at Williams Army Air Field was a former college football player and he was a decent and caring person. My flight and academic training went smoothly. The most difficult part was flying at night. When I made my takeoffs away from the lights of the city, it was eerily dark. I had to get accustomed to using my flight indicator to establish a horizon, but my training on how to transition from visual flight reference to instrument proved effective, so it went okay and I did not fall from the sky. However, one of my roommates crashed and was killed at night. The accident report indicated that he probably became disoriented immediately after takeoff.

When we reached the midpoint of our advanced flight training, our entire class was summoned to the base theater for a meeting with the Base Commander, Colonel Herbert Grills from my home state of Tennessee. He informed us that the Air Corps needed more bomber pilots to finish the war. The exceptionally heavy losses in Europe and the Pacific area were greater than projected. So the Air Corps had no choice but to transfer half of all the pilots in our class to bomber training. The tallest and largest pilots would be transferred to Las Vegas Army

Airfield and begin training to fly B-17 bombers.

Since bomber casualty rates were so heavy, the idea of moving to a bomber wing was frightening. In truth, flying anything in this war was risky. It just added to the anxiety level when you got moved into a higher risk assignment. Many guys I knew were very upset, but most took the news gracefully.

Those of us who remained at Williams were now required to take an additional thirty hours of flight training. That did not make a lot of sense to us, but not everything about the military always did. It was just that we now had the prospect of another round of reassignments to bombers if the casualty rates continued at a high level.

I completed fifteen more hours of flight training and garnered sufficient confidence to order my dress uniforms. When I saw that I was close enough to the end of training to feel confident about a graduation date, I invited Dad, Mother, my sister Opal and Hazel to attend my graduation and commissioning as an officer in the Army Air Corps. It was a bittersweet moment for my family. Perhaps in some small way this would lessen our grief over the loss of my brother Ralph.

Although gas and tires were rationed, I hoped they could be there for my graduation. I reserved rooms for my family at the Westward Ho Hotel in Phoenix. Determined to make it to my graduation on time, Dad drove his 1939 Chevrolet from Tennessee to Arizona in three and a half days. While Hazel was there, we talked about getting married. We had discussed the subject in our letters but had not made any decisions.

I did not have any idea where I would go after graduation. Usually, the Air Corps allowed graduates to have a short leave before reporting to their next assignment. However, three days after graduation, I received orders to attend gunnery training at Ajo, Arizona for three weeks, then to report to Luke Army Air Field, northwest of Phoenix, for P-40 flight training. By the time I got my orders, my family was already on their way back to Tennessee. I would not get leave until after I completed the P-40 training. At least I now had some idea about my immediate future.

Now that the excitement of graduation was over, I began to appreciate the status of my new position as a lieutenant. I felt proud as I moved around the base and got saluted by the airmen. I realized from that moment on that I would be expected to assume the responsibility for leading other men whether fellow officers or enlisted. First and foremost, I was expected to be an officer and a gentleman.

I had time on my hands after I arrived at Luke Field since there were many pilots waiting to accumulate flying hours and there was a shortage of airplanes available. It would take an inordinate amount of time for me to get the required one hundred hours in the P-40.

Shortly after Christmas, I was given fifteen days of

leave. I traveled by train to Tennessee to see my family. I called Hazel, who was now in Florida with her family, to talk about plans for our marriage. Hazel's family had to shut down the dry cleaners in Knoxville since they had no gas for pick-up and delivery, thanks to rationing, and her father was called up to work in the shipyards in Panama City, Florida.

Before I went to Florida to see Hazel, I first wanted to talk to Dad about getting married. Even though I was twenty-one years old, Dad had some reservations about us getting married since Hazel was only seventeen and the future was so uncertain. He recommended that we wait until after the war ended, but we wanted to get married before I finished my combat crew training. I did not get his full support to marry.

I left Knoxville by bus for Panama City to see if I could convince Lewis and Lola Ketner that I would be a good son-in-law. As I traveled I was thinking of all the positive reasons why they should approve of me. I did not want to think of anything negative.

I started the bus ride feeling optimistic about the outcome. At the same time, I felt that Lewis would have reservations because of Hazel's age and she was their youngest child. Her departure would leave them as empty nesters. Lola was soft hearted and I felt I could convince her that I was worthy of her daughter.

The more I thought about how to approach the subject the more my stomach churned. I just hoped that Lewis had a good day at the shipyard the day I would be talking to him. That would make the conversation much easier.

When I arrived, Lewis was in a good mood and Lola was busy cooking the evening meal. I was as nervous as a cat while we gathered around the table for dinner. After we ate, with much trepidation, I broached the subject about our getting married. To my pleasant surprise and with little discussion, both of Hazel's parents approved of our marriage. Lewis even offered to take a day off to go with us to get our marriage license.

As we drove through Panama City, I saw the beautiful First Baptist Church so I asked if we could stop so I could talk with the minister. I went to a Baptist church when I was younger, so I decided to ask the minister if he would marry us. I could hardly believe the good fortune I was having when he agreed to marry us in his study that same day at four o'clock. He understood that I only had a few days until I had to be back in Arizona.

I bought a beautiful corsage for Hazel, and Lewis and Lola stood by us as we repeated our vows of love for one another. I was so nervous that I cannot remember whether or not I gave the minister an honorarium. I think I did, but if I did not, I hope he has forgiven one fighter pilot whose knees were knocking all through the ceremony.

We left that night and rode a bus to Knoxville. We had only two days together before I left on a train back to Phoenix. Hazel planned to stay in Knoxville for a few days and then return to Panama City to her job. It was not a honeymoon made in heaven, but we were so excited to be committed to each other that we would have been happy on an Army cot back in good old Biloxi.

The train ride back to Phoenix passed rather quickly and I slept sitting up most of the way. There were few sleeping cars available during the war and they were above a 2nd Lieutenant's pay grade.

The train cars banged and slammed as their couplings adjusted to the sudden slowing when the train pulled into the station at Phoenix. I was startled from my sitting sleep position to realize I was back in Hanoi. The noises that shocked me back to reality were from the guard slamming my cell door open.

# Chapter 12

The guard tossed a maroon and gray striped prison uniform on the floor along with a pair of Ho Chi Minh sandals. I had great difficulty buttoning the jacket and tying the drawstring on the pants. The sandals were made from an old automobile tire with two pieces of rubber tube across the toes. I had heard stories from infantry soldiers about tracking Viet Cong soldiers by the tire tracks they left on paths. My feet were swollen beyond belief and I had trouble getting the sandals on.

Once I was dressed and wearing the crude shoes, the guard led me from the cell. I noticed that rats had finished eating the broth from my now empty bowl. It was not uncommon to see rats the size of cats or small dogs scurrying along building and bunker walls in Cam Ranh Bay and Da Nang so it was not surprising to me that they were residents of the Hanoi Hilton.

People were moving about the camp even though it was still before sunup. It had evidently started raining while I was sleeping so the guard gave me a yellow rain slicker and motioned for me to put it on. In a surprising gesture, he rolled up my pants legs and pulled the hood of the slicker over my head. Instead of returning to Room

106

18, he led me through puddles in the courtyard to the main prison gate.

Guards stationed at the gate swung one of the heavily wired doors open and my guard led me across the street to a stately looking government building I soon learned was the Ministry of Justice. It was an attractive and typically French structure with brushed stucco walls and tile roofing. A wall about six feet high surrounded what was once a well landscaped lawn. Several Vietnamese men were walking around on the grounds in their undershirts and shorts.

The guard led me around the exterior of the building to an entrance on the east side. It surprised me that I was allowed to be seen as I drew a lot of stares from the Vietnamese citizens. People were moving about doing their morning chores as I stumbled through the doorway with great difficulty. Once inside, I saw that the rooms were sparsely furnished with a few chairs and a table or two.

I was placed in a small room on the north side of the building. The guard abruptly departed closing the door behind him without giving me further instructions or directions. I thought about trying the door to see if it was locked but decided I would be pressing my luck if caught, so I went to the window to look outside. To my disappointment, all I could see were trees and bushes. I hoped to see a scene of damage and destruction from the bombing raids I had been hearing.

The door rattled open and my usual three interrogators marched into the room. They began with the same questions and my answers were the same. They then surprised me by asking if I knew Robbie Risner. I had not anticipated that the Vietnamese would ask me about another American prisoner.

I thought quickly how I would answer. I knew Robbie well. He was a student at the Air War College in 1961 while I was a student at the Air Command and Staff College. Years later, while I was studying at the National War College in 1966, I learned that Robbie had been promoted to full Colonel. Robbie had an outstanding combat record and was a superb F-105 squadron commander. He deserved the promotion.

Robbie was shot down and captured in September of 1965. He was an ace from the Korean War and was featured on the cover of TIME magazine. He was a charismatic guy and a great combat leader. Robbie had been shot down once before but was picked up by our rescue forces.

I also knew that Robbie had been flying combat missions from a base in Thailand and the official U.S. position was to deny that American pilots were using Thai airbases. Such a position placed a pilot shot down over North Vietnam in an untenable position. On the one hand, the American media was filled with reports of U.S. Air Force activity in Thailand. On the other hand a pilot could not admit he was flying out of Thailand. This was one of the many inconsistencies of U.S. policy.

I was vague in saying that I had met Robbie several years ago, but he probably would not remember me. I wanted to protect him in case he was using a cover story.

The interrogators then placed American magazines on the table including TIME, LIFE and U.S. News and World Report. I noticed that LIFE magazine had a cover story on an Air Force Squadron stationed in Da Nang, South Vietnam. The U.S. News and World Report magazine was dated April, 1967. The interrogators explained that the U.S. magazines were brought to North Vietnam by American peace (anti-war) groups. I felt disgust that Americans had committed acts of treason by providing aid and comfort to the enemy by collaborating with them and giving them propaganda information to use against us.

The remainder of that day was spent trying to convince me that I should cooperate with the Vietnamese in trying to bring the war to an early end. I would not enter into political discussions with them. Even when they threatened me with continued torture and punishment for failing to cooperate, I refused to take part in these discussions. I repeated again and again that I fully supported my government and its policies.

I guessed that bringing me to the Ministry of Justice Building to interrogate me was their way of threatening me with criminal proceedings if I did not cooperate. If they decided to put me through their version of a fair trial they could end up hanging me.

The change in venue was disquieting and did add a new element of fear for me. On top of that, the building was infested with huge mosquitos that feasted on my open wounds as well as the rest of my unclothed skin. My infantry soldier friends I saw occasionally in Cam Ranh Bay would joke that the mosquitos were so big that they did not eat you on site but would take you home to share with their families. These must have been of that variety.

I could not feel them on my feet, but when I looked down, they were already loaded with blood. I smashed and killed them all day long. The interrogators did not seem to be bothered with them. I began to think that this was another dirty Communist trick…they wanted me to catch malaria and die.

I was taken to the Ministry Building for three more days in a row, shackled on the floor and repeatedly interrogated. They asked the same questions over and over and took notes of my answers, hoping to catch me changing my stories.

Each night they took me back to Room 18 to interrogate me some more before providing me with a rice straw mat and a mosquito net to cover me while I slept. I could hear a person coughing throughout each night in an adjacent room. I hoped it was not an American.

On the fourth and last day returning from the Ministry, the guard escorted me to Room 18 and locked the door behind him. To my surprise, I saw a wicker basket containing American flying suits that had been left in a corner of the room. I was not in any condition to run but I made my best effort to get to it quickly. I frantically began to pull them out and search for name tags. I was desperate to see if I could identify any names belonging to the suits. I was horrified to think that more of our pilots had been shot down. Before I could find any name tags, a guard ran in, grabbed the basket and hustled it out of the room. A sense of rage and disappointment overcame me as I realized I had failed to learn anything about my fallen American comrades.

The guard returned shortly and led me out of Room 18 into the open courtyard. He began walking at a normal pace and I had difficulty keeping up. My battered body and bloodied feet and ankles made walking at all a tortuous endeavor. The fifty yards to the end might as well have been a marathon. I was determined to stay with him despite the pain.

The guard approached a large wooden door and swung it open to reveal a cluster of eight small cells. He led me to the last cell on the left side. The cell was about seven feet square with a concrete bed on each side. Seeing the two beds gave me a surge of hope that they might be intending to place me with a cell mate.

One large window partially covered with bamboo wattle at the bottom was across the cell from the door. The wooden door was about three inches thick with large iron hangers on the outside. I could see that it matched the other cell doors in the cluster. A small window that opened like a little metal door was in the center of the upper portion of the door. This was my introduction to my room in what was referred to as the "Heartbreak Hotel", where the severely injured and non-cooperative prisoners were kept.

A small piece of paper was posted on the inside of the door outlining the camp regulations. They were ridiculous! According to the regulations, I was not a prisoner of war but rather a war criminal. It stated that as a war criminal I had no individual rights. It instructed me to answer all questions truthfully and not communicate with other Americans. The camp regulations made it clear to me that the North Vietnamese had no intention of complying with the Code of Conduct under the Geneva Convention. I could envision ongoing trouble and torture for me since I knew there was no way I would comply with what I was reading.

The guard closed and locked the ominous wooden door behind him. I then heard the echoing sound of the main exterior door to the cell cluster slamming shut. It sounded like the heavy steel lid of a dumpster slamming down.

I looked around. At the end of each of the concrete beds was a set of iron leg stocks. The walls of the prison cell were about fifteen inches thick. No doubt, these cells had seen lots of misery. The floor was caked with grime and filth and appeared to have never been cleaned or scrubbed. Beneath one of the concrete beds was a smelly black bucket. I was disgusted to realize that this nasty pail was to be my toilet.

There was no communication from my captors to indicate what each stage of my treatment meant to me. I was led from one place to the other, interrogated, tortured and fed as one might feed a stray dog. I could only guess whether my current surroundings would be my permanent cell or just another stage in the multi-layered mistreatment process.

The cell I was in reminded me of the holding cages I remembered seeing at a dog pound. Now I knew how those stray or abandoned dogs felt as they sadly watched you walking around free on the outside. I was truly trapped and, like those unfortunate dogs, I had no idea what lay ahead. I could be euthanized like a stray dog without representation or due process.

My interrogators had constantly drilled me to acknowledge that my country had abandoned me by allowing me to be held prisoner by my enemies. It was part of the effort to break me, make me feel isolated from the world I knew and weaken my resolve to resist their efforts.

I needed to get off of my aching feet so I carefully lay down on the concrete bed on the left side of the narrow room. It hurt to get prone because it put pressure on my lower back where I had been repeatedly beaten. It hurt to try to lay on my side because my bloodied and raw ankles and feet touched each other and the pressure of the concrete on my knees made me wish I had more fat on my body for padding. My shoulders ached from the disjointing caused by the brutal torturing equipment. It was equally painful to me when they roughly popped my shoulders back into joint each time.

Now that they had secured me away in a cell, I wondered what would become of me. The last few days moving me from torture chamber to interrogation room to the Ministry of Justice had not given me much time to think about more than just the immediate future in terms of minutes, not days, months or even years. It was a relief that I was not being tortured or constantly pressured and coerced to give military information. However, I was somewhat surprised and disappointed that I had been put in solitary confinement.

When I was first captured, I was naïve enough to think that maybe I would be put in a cell or cellblock where I could see or talk to someone like my good friend Swede Larson who had been shot down a week before I was. No such luck. Because of my refusal to cooperate with the interrogators, I now stood a better than average chance to be in solitary confinement for a long time.

What the hell did it matter? If that were the only price I had to pay in order for me to maintain my honor and integrity and remain faithful to my government and its policies, it would be well worth it. Being in solitary would certainly not be pleasant, but to me the alternative was just not acceptable. I was determined not to give an inch.

Now at least I had a chance to pause and reflect on my situation and consider some options. If they could not get military information from me, they would probably try to coerce me into taking part in their propaganda programs. I had to guard against being duped as some Americans had been.

I had to put aside my personal feelings and act as if it did not matter whether or not I wrote to my family. In reality, more than anything else, I wanted to let Hazel and our sons know that I was alive and in fairly good shape after the torturing. If I asked for permission to write to my family or if I insisted they abide by the Geneva Convention regarding my treatment, they would take it as a sign of weakness.

I attempted to fool myself into believing that the prolonged torture and interrogation sessions were over. I recognized the negative effect the dread and fear that accompanied the sessions had on my ability to maintain cognizant thought processes. So, denial was the natural defensive mechanism. It was imperative that I steel myself to resist the temptation to break even the slightest amount. They would see even a miniscule crack in my determination as a sign of weakness and use it as an excuse to intensify their cruel techniques.

Bug liked to brag to me that his government had a lenient and humane policy for treatment of "American criminals." I imagined what it might be like if I could meet visiting delegations and expose the extreme conditions and torture we actually endured. I would challenge them to investigate violations of the Geneva Convention by Bug and his cohorts.

I had to face up to the fact that I was in solitary confinement and had to make the best of a bad situation. I had never been one to be a "Monday morning quarterback" or to play "what if". That is not to say that I never spent time looking back at the events of my life trying to decide what caused me to fail at times.

It is human nature to question our failures as compared to our successes in life. My current situation put me in a mindset to think too negatively and self critically. As I sat reviewing my life failings of things I had done that did not turn out as well as I intended, I mentally punished myself for not living up to my own expectations.

At some point in my emotional downward spiral it occurred to me that this self-questioning was exactly the effect my captors wanted to have on me. I then became determined to fight back and forced myself to turn to positive thoughts.

It had always been my belief that failure does not mean that life is over, that all is lost or that we can never recover. It means only that under pressure of the moment, we have failed to meet our own expectations. The hallmark of quality is that we have done our very best. The ultimate hallmark is failing but having the will to bounce back and fight again.

I reminded myself that I placed high standards on my personal and professional life. When I decided to pursue a military career, I was determined to be the best possible military officer that I could be.

My personal conduct and my dealings with other officers and officials were based on one major tenet; honesty. That was the way I was reared and I would never compromise my integrity for personal gain. I worked hard to be a good pilot, a good staff officer, a good student and a good representative of the Air Force. When I served in foreign countries or represented the United States at international meetings, I worked hard to be a good ambassador of the American people and our way of life.

Looking back and acknowledging my personal integrity helped me to clear my head and focus. So, as I waited in the cell and pondered my fate, I went back over the details of my flight. Our start engine time was 1430 hours and take-off was to be at 1500 hours. After starting the engines on my aircraft, the left generator would not come on line. I rechecked the switches, in accordance with normal operating procedures, and had to shut down both engines. The crew chief quickly checked the aircraft and assured me that he had never experienced that problem before. He suggested I start the engines again and cycle the generator switches through a couple of times. I did this and everything worked normally.

I radioed my flight leader who had already taken off

and told him I would join him at the refueling rendezvous point over Laos. The entire flight had refueled by the time I arrived so I slipped behind the KC-35 tanker and took on a full load of fuel. Shortly afterward we joined with the F-105's and F-4's from Thailand and headed due east for our target which a boat factory on the outskirts of Hanoi. All of the systems in my aircraft worked normally so I had no reason to believe that the aircraft or its systems played a significant role in my being shot down.

What then could I or should I have done differently to avoid being shot down? The sequence of events happened so quickly that I do not believe I could have done anything that would have altered the outcome. I suspected that debris from the SAM that missed us but exploded nearby got sucked into my engine and negatively affected my power. That would have been to blame for my inability to keep pace with the rest of the flight. Jim and I had carefully laid out alternative routes to use that would have helped us avoid known flak and SAM locations in case we had to leave the flight because of an emergency, but those plans became useless once our aircraft was crippled.

We had rolled the dice, as I had done on seventy-two missions before, and our number came up. So there was no reason to play "what if". Lady Luck ran out on us and the wheel of misfortune called out our number. Now it was time for me to look to the future and forget about the circumstances that landed me in this miserable place. One of the most important lessons I learned at the survival school was to maintain a positive attitude about the future and not to feel sorry for myself. Everything is relative. I was alive and in fairly good physical condition. Things could be worse.

I thought about Andersonville, Stalag Luft, Corregidor and the Korean prisons of just a few years ago. On balance, I reckoned that with His watch and care, I would survive this experience and it could become a positive force in my life. I suppose that, in reality, I was finding it necessary to reaffirm my faith in God, my faith in myself, my faith in my country, my faith in my fellow prisoners and, lastly, my faith in my family. The strength that seems to come from adversity and the determination to survive the most primitive conditions are qualities that perhaps we will never understand. It was now time for me to suck it up and to live up to the finest traditions of the American fighting man.

There was never any doubt in my mind what my role needed to be. I was still a combatant and I had to use every weapon I could find to harass the enemy. It was out of character for me to lie, steal or cheat. I was reared not to do these things. But now I intended to be just as devious and deceptive as I could be. I think that this was a defensive mechanism brought about by my giving in to the torture and giving information other than name, rank serial number and date of birth, even though the information I gave was largely fabricated and useless to them.

I knew that I had given them only trivial or misleading information that was readily available through the news or print media, so it would not be accurate to say that they broke me. I could still say that I had defied them and had not given them anything of substance.

Nonetheless, I had provided more than just the information required by the Geneva Convention to get them to stop the torture, so I could not live up to my own expectations and it bothered me. I had an empty feeling in the pit of my stomach, an emotional emptiness. I had compromised my principles and the only way I could justify my actions was on the basis of protecting my sanity and my physical wellbeing.

# Chapter 13

Since I was going to be in solitary confinement, at least for the time being, I would have to use all of my faculties to understand what was going on around me. I could use my sense of smell and my hearing to help me. The stench coming from the area outside of my cell told me that there must be an open trench nearby where prisoners emptied their buckets.

I could hear some Vietnamese voices just outside my window. Since I was not in the leg stocks today, I stood up on the concrete bed, but even with standing on my tiptoes, I could not see outside. I needed at least another eighteen inches to get to where I could look through the bamboo wattle.

I looked around the cell and saw that the walls had recently been whitewashed. I carefully scanned the walls and ran my hands across the surface to see if I could find any prisoner names or dates scratched on them. I found a lot of marks and scratching, but no names.

I lifted the iron leg stocks on one of the beds by using my leg to pry up the end of the metal bar. My heart leapt. Here was a note. I unfolded the paper and saw a calendar for several days in April and early May. Each day had been "X'ed" out. The person who had been in this cell was captured in April and he had been here until May 5th.

As I stood looking at the makeshift calendar, the small metal peephole in my door opened and there was Pigeye. He unlocked the door quickly and grabbed the paper from me. He mumbled disgustedly, convinced that he had stumbled upon something really important. He left the cell in great haste and I never saw the paper again.

Excited at having discovered evidence left by someone before me, I continued to scour every inch of the cell, all around the ceiling and under the bunks. I carefully dragged my fingers, though excruciatingly tender, on the floor along the perimeter of the tiny room. Near a dark corner of the exterior wall I discovered a small hole that I could slip my forefinger into if I lay on my side and maneuvered my body so my head was flat against the floor.

There was a greasy appearance to the concrete on the wall around the hole. I managed to manipulate the hole with my fingernail and was rewarded with crumbles of sand and concrete each time I withdrew. I looked along the wall on either side of the hole and saw the same greasy appearance I had discovered directly around the opening. That is when the realization hit me that my discovery was the hole the rats used to access my cell and eat my food leavings. The grease along the wall was evidence of a rat run.

I continued to prod the opening and was rewarded with

more sand and bits of gravel until I could fit my hand into the hole. I carefully withdrew my hand and pressed my face tight against the floor until I was delighted to see light. I sat up and studied my position in the room to orient myself and found that the rat hole opened into the prison courtyard. I was surprised at how elated I became at this small discovery.

Every day the routine was the same. At about five in the morning, the outside would come alive with voices and activity. A loudspeaker system would blare with oriental music followed by some Vietnamese dialogue. The tone of the speeches sounded to me like they were intended as motivational propaganda to propel the people to work harder and help defeat the United States. I could occasionally recognize the word "Johnson".

Following the speech making each morning, at around six or six-thirty, I could hear the loud counting of cadence in Vietnamese. Judging from the movement of shadows that I could see by lying on the floor and peering through the rat hole, it appeared that the guards and perhaps even the prisoners were taking exercise. Strain as I might, my hole was too low to the floor for me to be able to actually see people. Movement from their shadows and communication among them, though not clear enough to understand, was enough to give me hope that I might soon be among them.

Once the early morning activities ended I would hear the sounds of cell doors opening and closing. I imagined the guards were escorting prisoners to empty their buckets into the waste trench and returning them to their cells. There would be a blessed but brief period of quiet before the interrogation sessions would resume. One at a time, I could hear the shuffling footsteps of prisoners being hastily led away by guards. It was agonizing to sit listening intently until they would be returned, often to the sound of their legs dragging along the floor.

Each day the fruitlessness of the routine became more disheartening. I knew I would be the last to be taken to Room 18. The same three interrogators continued to question me. The approach of the interrogators became less violent as they altered their strategy from torture to mental deception and trickery while distorting realities and facts. They used clever tactics. They would describe statements they claimed one prisoner made then rapidly switch to contradicting assertions from another prisoner. I listened intently, but tried to convey the appearance that I really wasn't interested in what they were saying.

During the third week of interrogation, I stumbled upon an opportunity to play my own mind games. While in a one-on-one session with the oldest and largest of the three interrogators who I suspected might be Chinese, he began to discuss the Taiwanese support for the United States and how much money we were spending there in return. He referred to them as "American Lackeys". I casually mentioned that I had been to Taiwan many times although I had actually only been there twice. I told him I was strongly impressed by their armed forces and that the U.S. had to maintain control over them to prevent them from attacking China.

The interrogator took the bait. He shrugged his shoulders and, trying to sound nonchalant replied, "They are nothing but paper tigers!" I responded by saying that if the U.S. pulled the Seventh Fleet out of the Formosa Strait, Taiwan would conquer China in three weeks' time.

He was absolutely furious with me. He stammered and stuttered and got red in the face. I was now certain that he was Chinese. I had bested him and he lost face with me. His anger turned to rage as he proceeded to beat me about the head and face. He was humiliated and did not take it well. He was never the same as an interrogator. I would only see him a couple of times after that incident.

I was usually taken back to my cell by about 10:30 or 11:00 AM. The food would already be portioned out and left sitting on a small bench in the hallway. Sometimes it was covered with an enamel bowl or plate. Other times it was left open and the rats, huge ones, would be having part of it when I walked in.

Our meals normally consisted of a bowl of cabbage soup and a loaf of French style bread about eight to ten inches long and two inches in diameter. Occasionally, we got a bowl of rice instead of bread. Even though it had been cooked, odious small white worms would be crawling around in the rice bowl. I'm certain that I ate some of them, but never intentionally. It gave me a serious case of diarrhea and bleeding from the rectum.

I learned in survival school that lime could be used to treat diarrhea. I took my enamel drinking cup and flaked some of the whitewash paint off the wall and added water from my jug. After letting it soak for several hours, I drank the mixture.

# Chapter 14

At the end of my third week of interrogation, Bug and his interrogators were growing increasingly impatient with me and the guards slapped me in the face at every opportunity. I was not meeting their expectations in my Communist re-education program.

Many morning and afternoon interrogation sessions were nonproductive for them and they clearly resented the lack of cooperation. During this same time the bombing was becoming more intense giving me renewed determination with each strike. In addition to the usual morning and afternoon missions and much to my pleasure, our guys were now making some night attacks on Hanoi.

After each interrogation session I looked forward to returning to my cell and to my world of memories and dreams. I learned to cherish my solitary confinement time. It was far better than any exposure I had to human beings, if you wanted to call them that. I reached a point in my withdrawal from humanity where it irritated me to have my "solitary" time interrupted by the guards. Reliving my experiences and emotions both comforted me and sustained my will to survive.

My personal situation was growing worse. I had one set of prison clothes, a rice straw mat, a mosquito net, the enamel drinking cup, a ceramic water jug and a stinking black bucket for a toilet. The wounds on my ankles and legs were infected and I had practically no use of my hands. On top of all that, my diarrhea persisted.

As I thought about my situation and my treatment, I realized that I had slowly and deliberately been reduced to the level of an animal. No one in a civilized country would treat a person this way. This only caused me to strengthen my resolve to resist those bastards.

During my fourth week of captivity, the daily interrogations ended. One morning, the cell door opened and there stood a small Vietnamese man in an Army uniform and white jacket. He was friendly and seemed to be embarrassed as he looked at my physical condition. He examined my arms and hands, rolled my lower eyelids down and then pulled up my pant legs to examine my shins. He became visibly upset when he saw the wounds on my ankles and legs.

He talked rapidly to the guard who accompanied him and then asked me, in broken English, "Sleep well? Eat well? Sick?"

I motioned that I had diarrhea by pointing to my rear end and the smelly bucket. He nodded that he understood. The odor from my clothes and the bucket should have told him enough. He re-examined my legs and pressed on my shins until tears came to my eyes and then he stopped. He said one word, "medicine." I said "no penicillin" as I had previously experienced severe reactions to penicillin. He repeated "no penicillin" and left.

A couple of hours later, a young medic came into the cell carrying a medical kit. He had the kindest face I had seen in weeks. I could see in him a likeness to my older son, Steve, who at one time wanted to be a doctor. After spending several nights and weekends on duty at Duke Medical Center, he had decided that his future was not in medicine.

The young medic was extremely careful as he cleaned and dressed my wounds. For the first time, I met a Vietnamese who had genuine compassion for another human being. Neither of us spoke as he worked, but his warm smile convinced me that he was a good man. He applied a colloidal like substance to the open wounds on my legs and right arm. He also wrapped my left leg and ankle in gauze.

He appeared apologetic about my treatment and my condition. Before he left, he handed me two white tablets and pointed to my drinking cup. I smelled the tablets and asked, "Penicillin?" He did not respond. I was fairly certain it was penicillin, but I swallowed the tablets anyway. He packed his medical kit and in a symbolic manner, he bowed and left the cell. That was my introduction to "Tonto", a real professional and a person I saw three more times during my stay at the Hanoi Hilton.

The next day, I had large watery blisters come up on

the bottoms of both feet. The pills were in fact penicillin and this allergic reaction had happened to me once before. Now walking was nearly impossible. I had to hobble along on the outsides of my feet. The pain was excruciating. I could not break the blisters and the guards apparently did not think the medics should be told about my condition. After about ten days, the blisters burst and I began to walk better.

During the time that I was unable to walk, I sat on the concrete bed and pondered my future. I had a lot of time for introspection and I did a lot of deep personal examination. I had never done that before, at least not to the same degree as I did for those several days. No doubt, my self-evaluation was related to my spiritual beliefs and experiences. I realized that only after I reaffirmed my belief in God and in myself could I dwell on my future as a prisoner of war.

I tried to recall every detail of my interrogation; the questions, the political monologues by the Bug and the interrogators, and even the facial expressions of all the Vietnamese with whom I had contact. Even though I was working with a very small sample, I had to conclude that the Communist party in North Vietnam was willing to sacrifice everything and practically everyone in North Vietnam in order to gain control in South Vietnam. They were a tenacious enemy who would not give up simply because the U.S. was bombing them with our fighter airplanes. We had to increase the weight of our efforts by using more airplanes or resort to the use of our bombers if we wanted them to come to the bargaining table.

They were prepared to fight a protracted war on their terms. In the long run, they reasoned, the American people would not support a long, drawn out war. They also believed that the war was not supported by the majority of the American people based on news reports and visits they received from American war protesters.

America had committed its armed forces under questionable justification and to support a dubious government in South Vietnam. This was their assessment of the situation. Their words were emphatic as they boasted their defeat of France, one of the world's major powers, and they were determined to do the same to the United States. That was their goal and that was their battle cry.

I knew that following this line of thought was probably not healthy since it could lead me nowhere but into a state of depression. Nonetheless, my mind busily reviewed what I expected was the political situation in the U.S. and the decision-making process within our government. I came to the dreadful conclusion that the war would not end until at least 1969.

President Johnson did not have the political support necessary to undertake the massive military action needed to break the will of the North Vietnamese government. Even if he wanted to throw the full military might of America at the war, he would surely not embark on the effort until he was elected to a second term in the November 1968 presidential elections. That would be the best case scenario.

The worst case scenario was even more depressing. What if Johnson decided not to seek re-election or what if he was re-elected and died unexpectedly or was assassinated in his second term? If for any reason, Lyndon Johnson was not president in 1968, the next president would not do anything during his first term that would jeopardize his chances for re-election in 1972. That was a tough judgment for me to make but I made it based on my knowledge of our political system after having been exposed to it first-hand in Washington from 1961 to 1966. So, I surmised, the odds of the war ending in 1969 were slim to none and most likely not even before 1972.

I hobble-paced around within the confines of my seven foot long cell, now more worried than ever about my circumstances. When my captors allowed me to have this time to myself it opened up a can of brain worms for me that I now knew would haunt my every moment of confinement. I had to admit to myself that my odds of going home before I was fifty years old were growing slimmer with each passing day.

How I wished I could, in some way, influence decisions that would bring the war to a successful conclusion in the shortest possible time. We had the military capability to win. Why had we let it drag on and on? But, then I remembered a meeting on a Saturday morning in the Pentagon. The decision was being discussed that would limit the bombing of any target within twenty-five miles of the center of Hanoi. The protestors were screaming "Baby Killers" and the brass were listening. What would it be like to wait in this hell-hole for six, seven or even eight years knowing that it really wasn't necessary?

My thoughts turned to my dad. He was full of sage advice. One of his expressions was a favorite of mine, "plan for the worst, but hope for the best". That was all I could do now, just hope for the best. Once again I slipped into my dream world of memories.

# Chapter 15

I was back at Williams Army Air Field and getting frustrated because I was only allowed to fly about twenty hours in the P-40. At that rate it would take many months to get combat ready and I knew the war would not wait around for me. Something needed to be done. Somewhere in the chain of command a decision was made. About two hundred pilots would be sent to the Third Fighter Command in Florida to train in the long range P-51 airplane that would be used in the Pacific War. I was selected to be in that group of pilots. That was great news.

I pooled funds with three of the other guys being transferred to Florida and we bought a used car so we could use the allotted eight days to drive to our new base via Tennessee for home visits. Since Hazel and I would be allowed to live off base during the training, we had agreed that she would meet me in Knoxville so that she could see my family and drive with us to Tallahassee.

One of the guys wanted to stop in Nashville to visit his parents. The rest of us drove on to Knoxville and two of us stayed with my family. The fourth guy took a bus to Pennsylvania to pick up his car. Since we would have his car to complete the trip, I thoroughly cleaned our travel car and sold it in two days at Dad's service station. It worked out great because we were able to get all of our invested money back.

When our buddy came back through from Pennsylvania, we left for Tallahassee. Hazel and I were looking forward to our first opportunity since getting married for us to be able to live together as husband and wife. After getting Hazel settled in temporary quarters, we arrived only ten minutes before our sign-in deadline.

We immediately began training in P-51 airplanes. Then the Army announced that it would be receiving new P-51D's at bases throughout Florida. Most of the airplanes were diverted from shipments to Europe. We were transferred to Bartow Army Air Field in Bartow, Florida to fly the new planes. Hazel and I decided to live in Lakeland since housing was scarce in Bartow. We were fortunate to find a vacancy in an apartment building that was fully occupied by pilots from Bartow.

I was rapidly accumulating hours in the P-51 and knew when I reached the magic one hundred hours I would be shipping off to war. Hazel came home with exciting news in July that the doctor had confirmed she was pregnant. The due date was set for March of the next year, 1946. Being an expectant father added a new dimension to my responsibilities in life and I began to fret about not just having a wife but a child as well back home when I went off to war.

By the first of August, I had flown nearly one hundred hours in the P-51. I expected to complete my training by the middle of September. Then, on August 6, 1945, the world was shocked when our government announced that an atomic bomb was dropped on Hiroshima, Japan. Three days later a second atomic bomb was dropped on Nagasaki and the war ended a week later.

Three years, eight months and twenty-six days after the Japanese attacked Pearl Harbor, the war was over. During the war some fourteen million American men and women answered the call to serve their nation. Now America had to demobilize most of those who were in service.

Still classified as in training, I was offered an option for an immediate release from service or remain active until June 30, 1947. When I was commissioned as an officer, my commitment was for five years beginning November 20, 1944. It stated that I served at the pleasure of the President of the United States, so I guessed that meant they could recall me at any time.

I had accumulated almost five hundred hours of flying experience. What would I use that experience to do in civilian life? The job market would be flooded with pilots returning from war with far more flying time than me. And employers would be anxious to hire war heroes. So after long and hard consideration, Hazel and I opted to accept an immediate release from service. I was released from active service on October 5, 1945.

We moved in with my parents and I took a job with

Dad at the service station. I displayed the car that Hazel and I had bought at Bartow at the station and it sold right away giving me a small profit as I had predicted. Working with Dad proved to be an enriching experience. I had matured a lot since leaving home for the service and our relationship grew to one of mutual respect. I sincerely appreciated their help and support and I think Dad appreciated having me beside him at the station.

On Monday morning, March 4, 1946, Hazel delivered our son, Steven. He was my parents' first grandchild and he added brightness and love to our already close family home.

In the fall of 1946, I was summoned by the Air Corps to report to a base in South Carolina to be interviewed for a Regular Commission which would entitle me to serve indefinitely as a career officer. I had mixed emotions about being a career officer since I had made plans to get a college degree. At the same time, I knew attending college would be difficult because I had a wife and child to support.

I reported for the battery of tests and was interviewed by a board of officers. I passed all the tests and a physical examination, but the board felt I needed a college degree. I was disappointed when they rejected my full commission.

The following summer, I was summoned to another base in South Carolina for a second interview. They still wanted me to have a college degree. I felt like I was between a rock and a hard place without the ability to return to the military and insufficient funds to get a college degree. So, Hazel and I decided to bite the bullet and live on a shoestring long enough for me to get through college.

Hazel took a job as a payroll clerk for the City of Knoxville and I enrolled in a pre-med program at the University of Tennessee. We rented a small apartment and were squeaking by on her salary plus the little I made working twenty hours weekly while attending classes. Early in 1948, I scored an interview with Delta Airlines. But they wanted me to have multi-engine flying time.

It was a difficult time for both of us. With Hazel working and me working and attending school, there just did not seem to be enough time to dedicate to my studies and my grades reflected it.

Later that year, just as life seemed to be crashing down on us, like a gift from above, I received notice from the Army to once again appear before a board of officers in Fort Knox, Kentucky. This time they did not question my educational qualifications or my flying experience. They were very cordial and did not reject me. In fact, they wished me good luck. In less than six weeks, I received a letter directing me to return to active duty in February of 1949.

 My assignment would be for a three-year tour as a pilot in a fighter wing in Neubiberg, Germany, a suburb of Munich. I would travel to Germany and then request permission for my family to join me. I was astounded by the letter. It provided an unexpected solution to our difficulties. It was also exciting because neither of us had ever been outside of the United States.

Developments in the world were creating a need for military pilots. The Cold War with the Soviet Union was intensifying. The United States Air Force had been created in September of 1947 and they started recruiting experienced pilots in 1947 and 1948. It made good economic sense to activate trained pilots from the World War II era. Now I would be able to compete for a regular Air Force commission.

Although it meant forgoing my college degree, Hazel and I decided that taking this opportunity was best for us at that time. I reported for active duty to Camp Kilmer, New Jersey on February 14, 1949. On March 4, 1949, Steven's third birthday, I boarded The USS Gibbons along with four hundred enlisted personnel as well as women and children who were dependents of servicemen already in Europe. I quickly developed a comradeship with fifteen other Army Air Corps officers on board during the seven days it took to sail from New York to Bremerhaven, Germany.

I felt like I had boarded an emotional roller coaster. I was elated to be back in the service and questioned my intelligence for ever leaving. At the same time, I had never ventured outside of the United States and I was feeling the emptiness of leaving Hazel and Steven behind.

I was one of only two 2nd Lieutenants stationed at Neubiberg. The other was Charlie Ray from Memphis. I learned quickly that with my rank it was best to be seen instead of heard, so I was careful to keep a low and unassuming profile. I was assigned to the 86th Fighter Wing, one of two wings in all of Germany. It had a rich heritage and a legendary hard-drinking Commander. The wing was equipped with the infamous World War II fighters, the P-47 Thunderbolts.

Within a month of my arrival, I was checked out in the Thunderbolt and was feeling my way among the old timers. I was assigned to the Supply Squadron. Three months into my tour, as soon as I was allowed, I applied for my family to join me.

Things continued to get better for us as I was promoted to 1st Lieutenant on January 10, 1950, which was also our sixth wedding anniversary. With the promotion came reassignment from the Supply Squadron to the 525th Fighter Squadron where I wanted to be all along. I had almost unlimited opportunities to fly and amassed 619 hours in eighteen months, more than anyone else in our squadron.

Later in 1950, I was assigned to the 86th Fighter Group as a staff officer. I also did some planning for joint maneuver operations with the U.S. Army Forces in Europe. I was transferred back to the fighter squadron when our wing converted to jet aircraft. I qualified in the F-84E which I flew until I was grounded with a broken leg from a skiing accident in January of 1952. I was grounded for the last three months I was at Neubiberg, but I still managed to fly over 700 hours during my tour.

I was feeling a welcomed emotional high when my cell door banged open and the guard pointed to my disgusting bucket. It was time to visit the awful excuse for a sewage trench.

# Chapter 16

I was not interrogated for the next several days. Perhaps they had shot down and captured other American pilots and were interrogating them. I hoped that was not the case.

My days were now becoming routine. I would be awakened by the loudspeaker just outside my window at 5:00 AM. About two hours later, it would be sewage disposal time. The guard would open the cell doors one at a time and lead the prisoner to Cell Number 8 where he could empty his bucket in a trench. The cell was like the others except that it was used as a nasty latrine. The guards would visit it to urinate on the floor without cleaning up afterwards. Over time the odor became nearly unbearable.

The cell also served as a place for prisoners to bathe and wash clothes since it had a shower head and a water faucet on the outside back wall. On my daily visits to empty my bucket I hoped and prayed that I would be allowed to clean. I just did not happen to be that lucky. I was deprived of the privilege to bathe, shave or brush my teeth for over a month now. My mouth tasted like the bottom of a dirty bird cage. I must have looked like a vagabond.

Pigeye always yelled "quigly, quigly" as I emptied my bucket. Thanks to my injured hands, I had difficulty keeping a firm grip on my bucket and tended to drop it noisily as I went about the dumping process. My bumbling would anger Pigeye and he would slap me on the jaw or kick me in the butt as punishment.

I carefully listened each day to the number of cell doors being opened so I could guess how many prisoners were in our cell block. When Pigeye opened Cell Number 6, the cell next to mine, he almost always had a conversation with the person in there and the best I could tell their two-way conversation was in Vietnamese. So I assumed the prisoner was an ARVN soldier or South Vietnamese pilot.

When the food arrived about 9:00 or 9:30 and again about 2:00 or 2:30, Pigeye would take the person out of Cell Number 6 and he would portion out the food, leaving it on a small stand in the hall for us to retrieve. Once we had eaten, we took the enamel plates or bowls and the single utensil, a small aluminum spoon, back to the table. Pigeye would open Cell Number 6 again and the prisoner would wash the dishes in his cell and put them back on the table.

If for some reason Pigeye did not open the doors for us to take our bowls outside within a short time after eating, the rats would pay us a visit. They were huge, larger than ordinary squirrels. They fought over who would get the leftovers. I had as many as three of them in my cell at one time and it was a constant battle to try to run them out. The best I could do was cause a small commotion by shuffling my feet but they soon realized that, in my condition, I was truly harmless.

I was excited one day when I heard some English words spoken in Cell Number 6. I had only heard Vietnamese spoken with the guards from that cell previously. Emboldened by this discovery, when I thought the guards had left the area, I decided to try to communicate with the prisoner in the next cell. I was elated to learn that he spoke English and that we would be able to talk with each other. He informed me that he was a South Vietnamese pilot who had been shot down. I asked where he learned to speak English and he surprised me with news that he attended flying school at Randolph Air Force Base. He said the Americans nicknamed him "Max." Although we attempted to avoid discovery, the guards overheard us one day. As punishment, they tortured Max horribly, so we stopped trying to talk to each other.

One day I heard Pigeye speaking in a jovial tone to some Vietnamese girls. He opened my cell door and motioned for me to bring my ceramic water jug with me. I thought at first that I misunderstood his direction since I was not used to being allowed to have contact with anyone other than Pigeye and my interrogation crew.

Two girls in military uniforms were in the hallway

carrying a large container of boiled drinking water on a long wooden pole. The care they took to provide clean water was in sharp contrast to the obvious lack of sanitation used in the preparation of our filthy, worm and parasite infested soup, rice and bread.

Pigeye strutted around like a peacock enjoying his role as the chief of the cellblock. The girls he lorded over were about the least attractive Vietnamese women I had seen since being in country, but the presence of a woman, any woman, was a welcome change. The female gender to me represented a feminine tenderness human beings learn at an early age to associate with love, caring and family. Those emotions had been lost to me during my long periods of torture and brutality.

It was almost entertaining to watch the gruff and physically unkempt Pigeye's flirtations with the food and water service girls. But, his position in the camp must have been high enough to impress someone since he frequently rendezvoused with one of the girls in our hallway during the siesta hour. I was sure they were not discussing such mundane subjects as the Vietnamese Workers' Party and how to defeat the Americans.

Late one afternoon, Buff opened my cell door and tossed a long sleeved shirt and long pants in the middle of the cell floor and motioned for me to put them on. I worked as quickly as I could, but apparently not fast enough to suit Buff. He boxed me on the head several times and yelled at me. Buff was not very smart. He was playing with less than a full deck and he was mean to boot.

Finally, in desperation, he helped me to get my clothes on. Next, he blindfolded me and led me outside to the main courtyard. I could see the walkway, but I did not want him to know it. He guided me to a small truck then hoisted me up into the back and climbed in beside me.

I could feel the presence of other people in the back of the truck. The way this detail was carried out convinced me that I was in the midst of a firing squad and the people in the truck with me were my executioners. Holy smoke! Surely they would not have missed out on the pleasure of seeing me squirm after threatening me first. But if this was the way it was to be, then swell, sayonara and so long to everyone and everything that I loved. During periods of depression, especially in the middle of the night while sitting hunkered in the dark, I had convinced myself that the North Vietnamese would execute me when they became convinced they had all the information they would get out of me.

The truck engine started and we moved slowly through the gate and turned right. We went a short distance that took only a few minutes and after several more turns, the truck maneuvered to a stop before backing up. Buff took my blindfold off and I was excited to see that all of the soldiers were walking away without even looking back in my direction. I felt like I had truly dodged a bullet.

Buff ordered me to get out of the truck and walk into

the doorway of a wooden building that reminded me of our World War II era military hospitals. Hospital odors of cleaning solutions and rubbing alcohol confirmed for me that we were, in fact, entering a hospital. Vietnamese civilian patients crowded the waiting and admittance area and they looked at me first with curiosity and then animosity once they realized I was American.

My mind was racing after being convinced that Buff and his crew were taking me out to shoot me only to learn that I was actually about to receive medical attention. I worried that people around me could hear my heart pounding in my chest from the fear induced adrenalin rush.

Shortly, several uniformed men came into the room and began to examine me, more like a prize horse than a patient. They lifted my arms, manipulated my hands and fingers and turned me from side to side to examine the front and back of my body.

They moved me to an adjacent room equipped with some old medical traction and splint fixtures that looked to be from the 1940's. They studied my arms and appeared to be discussing ways to use the traction devices, making notes as they talked among themselves. When they finished, they gave the notes to Buff and we returned to the truck. I now saw that the truck we arrived in was a small, three-wheeled utility truck similar to ones I had seen in Europe and Northern Japan. Buff put the blindfold on me and we returned to Hoa Lo Prison.

Buff appeared about the same time the following day and motioned for me to put on the same pants and shirt again. The temperature in the cell must have been nearly a hundred degrees. Perspiration rolled off me even though I sat motionless on the concrete bed. I was not getting enough water and the loss of salt was causing me to have stomach cramps.

Buff prodded and screamed until I finally got my clothes on and we headed for the small truck. Even in my weakened condition, I took comfort this time in knowing we were headed for the hospital instead of a firing squad as Buff put the blindfold on me.

When we arrived we bypassed the waiting area and went directly to a small treatment room. A petite nurse in an army uniform came into the room and motioned for me to take off my shirt. I had great difficulty getting the buttons open so Buff intervened by slapping me in the face several times. He finally got frustrated at watching me fumble around and roughly took my shirt off for me.

Regardless of the terrible abuse and filth I had endured during captivity, I felt terrible embarrassment because of my body odor while in the presence of the nurse. I guess it was a positive sign that I was still able to muster some sense of pride. Keenly aware of the odor, I felt awkward as she sat down on a small stool near me and examined my hands and arms.

She removed six silver needles from a small metal box. The needles were extremely light gauge, very flexible and about three inches long. A coil of copper wire curled around four or five times at the end of each needle. She grasped my left hand and placed it on the table. She inserted a needle through the muscle between my thumb and forefinger. I was amazed that I did not feel any pain and there was no blood. She reached for my right hand and followed the same procedure, then rolled my hand over and inserted another needle in the area where you take your pulse. Next, she inserted a needle about two inches above each elbow.

I had never experienced acupuncture treatments. I rolled my hands over to look at my palms and I could see the needles sticking out about a quarter of an inch, yet I did not feel any pain. She motioned for me to remain still and left the room.

She returned half an hour later and began to stick the back of my hand with a needle, signaling me to tell her if I felt pain. I shook my head indicating that I did not feel the needle. She removed all of the needles and dropped them back into the metal box. I observed that she did not clean or sterilize them after use and wondered whose blood or possible diseases I had just shared.

The next night Buff took me back to the hospital for more treatments. I think he enjoyed showing off for the nurse as he slapped me around for not moving fast enough, just like the night before. I could not help thinking to myself what a pleasure it would be to reverse roles and slap and humiliate him the way he did me.

The nurse took me to a room with an old electrical therapy machine that I noticed was manufactured in Germany. She removed four thick bandages that appeared to be made out of canvas and wrapped one around each hand. She then took a bottle and poured a liquid solution over the thick bandages.

She wrapped the other two bandages around my arms just above the elbows and poured another type of solution on them. I tried to see the label on the bottle but she kept hiding it from me. She connected an electrical wire from the machine to each of the four bandages and turned on the machine, adjusting the current by turning a rheostat. The gauge was calibrated from 0 to 150. She increased the current to 40 and left it there for 30 minutes. She pricked my fingers occasionally to see if I had any feeling in them. I did not.

We returned to the hospital for electrical therapy treatments each night for ten days. On the last treatment, the current was increased to 100, yet I still had no feeling in my fingers.

During my last three visits to the hospital, I noticed a wall calendar with daily tear-off sheets. I had been keeping up with the date by scratching on the wall of my cell and I was confused when I saw that the tear-off date on the first day read June 9 when I had calculated it on my wall to be the tenth. I was relieved the next day to see that the date showed June 11, a small but rewarding acknowledgement that I had retained at least some presence of mind.

Since the acupuncture and electrical therapy both failed to return feeling to my hands, my captors decided on an even more provocative treatment regimen. Buff came into my cell carrying a large syringe and a needle that looked like a railroad spike. Holy smoke! Surely the medics did not trust Buff to give me a shot!

I managed to get a look at the vial. The label appeared to be in Russian so I had no idea what it was. So here I was, horrified that a guy I doubted could count to ten, was about to inject me with a drug that could possibly kill me and I was unable to resist. Buff pulled up my right sleeve and socked the needle in. He took great delight in torturing me with that big needle. It was a horribly painful experience.

I would have to endure twelve more daily shots from Buff, all with the same unsterilized needle. He took great pleasure as he sadistically made a grand gesture of administering the shots.

Buff was also assigned to demonstrate how I was supposed to place my hands against the wall to exercise my hands and arms to rebuild the torn muscles and ligaments. Buff was the kind of guy who could find a way to break an anvil with a rubber mallet. What he lacked in brains, he made up for in pure stupidity. But I gleaned enough information from his instructions to figure out the best exercises and they did seem to help.

Late in June, I was called out for more interrogation.

As I walked to Room 18, I saw a set of scales that were being used to weigh rice bags. I quickly stepped up on the scales before Buff could notice and saw that I weighed 55 kilos. Buff was enraged by my audacity and slapped me around furiously. He was several steps ahead of me and did not realize that I had stopped. By my calculation I weighed 121 pounds. I had lost 35 pounds in six weeks.

In the interrogation room, Bug really did not have much to say. He took out his little black book from his shirt pocket and gave a report on how the war was going. It was the same rhetoric filled with lies and distortions. The session was mostly for an attitude check on my part. No change. I was still not contrite.

Toward the end of the session, he said that he was concerned about my health. Yeah, right. If he really was concerned, he was not doing anything about it. He said that he would give me extra food. I was outraged and told him that I would not accept special privileges or extra food. I told him that others in the camp probably needed the extra food more than I did. I insisted that I would only accept the same food portion as everyone else received and the same applied to any other special treatment. I told him that in my cell block they should feed everyone else before giving me my portion. He seemed stunned by my comments.

In reality, there was no way I could tell what other prisoners were getting. It was important to me that he understood I could not be bought. The session ended and as I waited for the guard to take me back to my cell, I checked beneath the blue table cloth to see if he had recorded our conversation. I was disappointed to see that he had not.

There was not any extra food for me. I went out several times to confirm that all the bowls and plates had the same thing and the same amount. I hoped the other prisoners did not continue to experience the same extent of diarrhea and weight loss as me.

The days dragged on and I was interrogated every couple of weeks. Bug continually hammered me about my bad attitude. When I would not answer his questions or when I gave long, ambiguous answers that had nothing to do with the questions, he would say, "You are the dumbest Colonel I've ever seen. Even some of the Lieutenants are smarter than you." What a great compliment. At least my resistance was frustrating somebody in the camp.

With that satisfying realization, I sought comfort from my private thoughts on my less than comfortable bed.

# Chapter 17

It was the spring of 1952 and my three-year tour in Germany was coming to an end. Now that we were on the way home, I reflected on the good fortune that had befallen us now that we had returned to military life. We had gone from being a naïve young couple barely scraping by from one day to the next to seasoned world travelers cared for by a vast military family. Housing, food, medical care and even much of my clothing were provided for us and I received better pay than I could ever have imagined only a few years earlier. Little Tony, the latest addition to our family while we were in Germany, was flourishing.

We drove to our next duty station at Turner Air Force Base in Albany, Georgia. I was assigned to the 309th Squadron. I checked out in the F-84G model which was an updated version of the F-84E I flew in Germany. My operations officer informed me that I had been selected to attend a fighter weapons course in Las Vegas, Nevada. It was ten weeks in duration and I could take my family with me. We packed the few things we had with us, drove to Las Vegas and rented a furnished apartment near the base. I began classes immediately.

Upon completion of six weeks of training, I received a message that I was to return to Albany that same night. An airplane would arrive at the base at midnight to fly me and five other pilots to Turner Air Force Base. No explanation was given. Our families would have to return by themselves.

We bought a new car that very day but we did not have a license plate for it. Hazel would need to explain that to the license plate agency. Quickly, we developed a plan for her return to Georgia. We set up a daily time for her to call me. She would drive as many miles each day as she safely could. I would let her know what was happening at Turner if it was not classified.

She drove from Las Vegas to Albany in four and a half days. I was only allowed to tell her that I was going on a classified mission and would be gone three months. I did soften the news by sharing with her that I had been promoted to Captain.

The morning after I arrived at Turner AFB, my Squadron Operations Officer explained that I needed to qualify in air-to-air refueling. He briefed me on the procedures to refuel from a KB-29 refueling tanker with a flying boom. We would take off as a two-ship flight and he would demonstrate the procedure for me. Then I would need to do four successful hook-ups. As we reached the runway takeoff position, he informed me that he had problems with his aircraft and would not be able to fly the mission. He told me to rendezvous with the tanker and practice refueling on my own.

Thankfully, it was a fairly calm day and I completed the hook-ups without any difficulty. Air refueling is essentially flying in formation at the rear of a tanker aircraft. The boom is operated by an airman who can see the receiver aircraft. After the receiver pilot opens the refueling receptacle, the boom operator "flies the boom" over and inserts it into the receptacle. Fuel is then transferred from the tanker to the receiver. In turbulent weather, refueling is challenging.

When Hazel and the kids arrived in Albany, I was given the day off so that I could be with them. We went to a motel and I brought her up to date on what I had learned. Our fighter wing had been ordered to go to Japan for three months. While we were there, we would fly some classified missions. The startling news was that we would fly our airplanes across the Pacific, the first time single engine jet airplanes would accomplish that feat. That explained why I needed the airborne refueling capability.

Before Hazel and Steve left Albany for Tennessee, she bought a local newspaper. It provided all of the details about our classified mission including the bases in Japan. We were both surprised at the breach of military secrecy. The paper did mention that when completed, our flight would be an historic event, the first crossing of the Pacific Ocean by single engine jet aircraft.

The code name for the flight across the Pacific Ocean

was Fox Peter One, indicating that this was the First Fighter Project in the Pacific area. Our Commander, Colonel David Schilling, was the leader of sixteen P-80 jets that crossed the North Atlantic in 1948. His experience was reassuring to all of us.

On July 4, 1952, the first two jets from the 307th Squadron rolled down the runway for this historic flight. Colonel Schilling and his wingman, Captain Freddie Poston, would lead the flight with ten other pairs of fighters close behind. We were bound for Travis AFB, California. Before Colonel Schilling reached the Mississippi River, the entire squadron was in the pre-designated flight formation.

Thirty minutes after the preceding squadron was airborne, the lead airplanes of the 308th Squadron began their takeoff roll. Lieutenant Colonel Jerrold Vivian was the leader of his squadron of twenty-two airplanes. Thirty minutes after the last element of the second squadron lifted off, Major Haden Curry and his wingman rolled down the runway leading the 309th Squadron. All twenty-two of our airplanes took off on time.

The entire wing refueled at 15,000 feet altitude over the Wink, Texas radio beacon. There were sufficient tankers to support the entire operation. Having a thirty minute separation between squadrons, the operations went very smoothly. Two or three pilots had problems with their aircraft and landed at airfields in west Texas or in Arizona.

Approximately six hours and forty-five minutes after leaving Turner AFB, we landed safely at Travis AFB. The Flight Operations Center could not believe that we had flown twenty-five hundred miles without landing and refueling. We reluctantly admitted that we had refueled in the air.

Once everyone had landed safely at Travis, Colonel Schilling scheduled a major briefing for the next leg of our flight. There were two problems that we had to contend with. The first issue was the headwinds. The winds were too strong for us to reach Hawaii with only one refueling. The second issue was that our refueling point was at Weather Ship Nan, seven hundred and fifty miles from San Francisco. The tankers did not have sufficient fuel capability to remain on station for up to two hours as they did in Texas and still land safely. Accordingly, the operation was put on hold until the winds at altitude decreased. Furthermore, to provide safety for the tanker crews, only one squadron of fighters would pass through each day.

The first squadron led by Colonel Schilling took off for Hawaii on July 6th. All twenty-two airplanes proceeded to the refueling point. One or two pilots could not refuel successfully and the spares filled in. Colonel Schilling and his wingman both had refueling problems and had to return to Travis. Major Bob Keen, Commander of the 307th Squadron, led the remainder of the squadron into Hawaii. Colonel Schilling's airplane could not be repaired for twenty-four hours, so he remained at Travis an extra day and led the 309th Squadron.

The 308th Squadron left for Hawaii on July 7th. Two of their pilots had problems and returned to California. The spares filled in for them. Everyone arrived safely. The 309th Squadron, led by Colonel Schilling, lifted off for Hawaii at 9:00 AM on July 8th. Colonel William "Dinghy" Dunham was leading the second flight of four airplanes. I was flying the #3 position in the third flight. As I watched Colonel Dunham refuel, I observed and radioed that a long plume of fire was coming from the rear of his airplane. He disconnected from the tanker and lowered the nose of his aircraft to regain some airspeed to extinguish the flame.

He called Colonel Schilling and told him that he might have to bailout over the weather ship. I called my flight leader and told him that I would stay with Colonel Dunham during his emergency. As he circled down I saw another plume of fire coming out of his airplane. Thankfully, he was able to restart the engine. He called Colonel Schilling and told him he was heading for Hawaii.

I checked our fuel quantity and told Colonel Schilling we would need a tanker before we reached Hawaii. We had some seventeen-hundred miles to go and did not have enough fuel to reach there. Fortunately, the overall plan had a tanker on standby at Weather Ship Uncle which was 750 miles to the east of Hawaii.

We had to descend to 18,000 feet to refuel. I suggested to Colonel Dunham that he needed to maintain more airspeed as he refueled. Colonel Dunham was a distinguished, decorated hero of World War II, but he did not have much experience in jets so he appreciated my caution.

We landed about twenty-five minutes after the rest of the 309th Squadron. Upon examination of the engine in his aircraft, five of the nine burner cans had collapsed. Theoretically, the engine could not sustain level flight. That night at the bar, Colonel Dunham bought drinks for everyone.

The average flight time from California to Hawaii was six hours and forty-five minutes. Due to some malfunctions of the refueling system in the fighter aircraft, only fifty-nine airplanes completed the flight to Hawaii. The remainder of the journey would not require in-flight refueling.

Our route would take us to Midway Island, Wake Island, Eniwetok Island, Guam, Iwo Jima and then to Yokota Air base near Tokyo, Japan. Just repeating the names of these historic World War II battle sites was humbling, much less having an opportunity to see them. I knew that if I had managed to accumulate sufficient flight hours before the war ended I would likely have participated in bombing missions to some or all of them.

At Iwo Jima, Lieutenant Colonel Elmer DeRosa, one of the Wing's most experienced pilots, was forced to eject from his airplane when the engine failed. Unfortunately, his parachute malfunctioned and he was fatally injured. His death was a shock to every one of us.

On the final leg from Iwo Jima to Tokyo, we flew in a mass formation of fifty-eight airplanes. Within twelve days, the Thirty-First Wing had flown over ten-thousand miles.

General Otto P. Weyland, Commander of the Far East Air Forces, was on hand to greet us. The celebration of the accomplishment concluded with a special prayer and acknowledgement for Lieutenant Colonel DeRosa. After the welcoming ceremony, most of the pilots retired to the Officers Club for rest and relaxation.

Over the next three days the weather was extremely vicious so very few planes took off or landed at Yokota Air Base. When the weather improved, the 307th and 308th Fighter Squadrons flew into Misawa Air Base in Northern Honshu and the 309th Squadron went into Chitose Air Base on the island of Hokkiado. We remained on Hokkaido for three months before the entire 31st Wing returned to Turner AFB via commercial flights. Our aircraft and all of the support equipment were left in place as a deployment for our replacements, the 508th Fighter Wing, which had also been stationed at Turner.

I returned from Japan in late October of 1952 and our flight arrived at Turner AFB at two o'clock in the morning. There to greet me was my dear wife, Hazel, and our son, Steve. Our neighbor and friend, Sam Craig, was so concerned for Hazel and Steve's safety that he followed them in his car from the apartment to Turner to insure that they were there when I landed.

In 1953, the 31st Fighter Wing was awarded the Distinguished Unit Award and the Commander, Colonel David Schilling, was awarded the Harmon Trophy for planning and executing the historic flight from Turner to Japan. Unfortunately, Colonel Schilling was killed in a car accident in England five years later.

In January of 1953, I was sent to Kirkland AFB, New Mexico, to attend Nuclear Weapons School. Our fighter wing was selected to be a part of the Nuclear Strike Force equipped with small tactical weapons. While there I was given more information on nuclear weapons than I wanted or needed to know. On February 9, 1953 Hazel's father Lewis died suddenly of a heart attack. I was granted an emergency leave so that we could go to Knoxville and be with her family to attend his funeral services.

The rest of 1953 was a whirlwind of intensified training that sent me all over the place. In May, I was selected to attend the Squadron Officers' School at Maxwell AFB in Montgomery, Alabama. It was a six week course designed for Lieutenants and Captains. I was able to return home on the weekends since it was only a two-hour drive from Albany to Montgomery. Two other officers from the base were attending the course, so we were able to car pool. Like most junior officers, we each had only one car so we took turns rotating whose car we would use for the weekend trips.

In July, our squadron was sent to MacDill AFB in Florida for three weeks of gunnery training. In August, I went to a Survival Training School in the Okefenokee Swamp for one week. In September I went to Basic Survival Training in Nevada for ten days. Then in November, our squadron was placed on alert for a second deployment to Japan. Once again I would have to defer to Hazel to maintain our family while I was gone on a three-month tour of duty.

When I returned from Japan in February of 1954, I was concerned about the amount of time I was spending away from my family. I talked to my squadron commander and asked if I could be transferred to Europe for another three-year tour. I was seriously thinking about resigning from the Air Force when, in April, he called me in to tell me that he had a request for a person with my experience to go to England for a three year tour. It was mine if I wanted it. I jumped at the opportunity.

In the early part of May, I left for England. I drove to New York and turned in our 1952 Plymouth station wagon for shipment. Hazel was left with the responsibility of having our personal belongings and furniture packed for shipping to England.

I was assigned to the 81st Fighter Wing at Bentwaters, England. My duty station was at Sheppards Grove, about fifty miles from Bentwaters. Two of the 81st wing squadrons were located there and I was assigned to the

92nd Squadron as a pilot. The squadron was equipped with the F-86A airplanes. As soon as I could, I requested permission to have my family join me.

I checked out in the F-86 and developed an immediate fondness for the airplane. I wanted to fly it at every opportunity and quickly accumulated eighty-three hours of flight time. The daily routine missions only lasted an hour and twenty minutes so I was frequently airborne.

In the latter part of August, 1954, I was transferred to the Wing Headquarters as the Wing Standardization Officer. The wing was scheduled to receive new airplanes, the F-84F, in mid-1955. The Wing was designated as a part of the nuclear strike force in Europe. The new job meant that we would have to move closer to the wing headquarters at Bentwaters. I was sent back to Langley AFB, Virginia, to check out in the F-84F and help write an operating manual for the aircraft. I also traveled to Turner to talk to a group of their pilots about the new airplane.

In early March of 1955, I was informed by the Air Force that I was selected to be a Regular Air Force Officer, with a permanent rank of First Lieutenant. It was not a demotion or slap in the face. It was just the normal process since all promotions were termed "temporary".

Our new T-33 airplanes, flown in by Air Force pilots, began to arrive in the summer. Weather became a major factor in the execution of our mission. The weather across the North Atlantic is hazardous most of the time, so the pilots were often required to wait for suitable flight conditions. The weather in Britain was heavily overcast and at its worst during the fall and winter and that hampered the checkout program for the new airplanes. Although not related to weather, one of our pilots was killed in a tragic accident so our commander, Colonel Ivan McElroy, was reluctant to try checkouts in marginal weather conditions.

The Air Force decided to move the airplanes to an American airbase in Casablanca, Africa where the weather was much better. I flew with Colonel McElroy in a T-33 two separate times to review the transition training. Sadly, one of our most experienced pilots was killed in North Africa. The accident board believed that he was doing unauthorized maneuvers in the aircraft.

In October 1955, Colonel McElroy informed me that he had a request from Air Force Headquarters to transfer me to Wiesbaden, Germany. Although he attempted to decline the transfer in an effort to keep me in England, he later had to approve the transfer. Orders were issued and I was directed to report for duty in November.

This time I was allowed to stay behind and help Hazel get our things ready to ship. The U.S. Army would be providing all of our household furniture in Germany so we sold our furniture to other Americans. We were not allowed to sell or give anything to the British people.

In September of 1956, I was selected to go to Edwards Air Force Base in California to do some performance testing on a new airplane, the F-100D model. The test data would be part of the F-100D Flight Handbook. Our command would begin to receive the new aircraft in late 1956, and I would be one of the instructor pilots. I was not eager to be gone for a month, but I was the only tactical fighter pilot in our office. I flew from Wiesbaden to Washington, D.C. on the "Blue Plate Special," an aircraft that was reserved for General Officers traveling to meetings in Washington. It was pretty plush. I was not as fortunate on the flight from Washington to California.

In California, the desert was hot and dry during the day and cool at night. Like my time in Arizona, I had to wash one of my two flight suits every day. There were three pilots doing the flight tests, and we normally flew one mission each day. After collecting the flight data, we passed the information to the aeronautical engineers and they analyzed it and developed performance charts for the new aircraft.

I met and worked with famous test pilots Chuck Yeager, Deke Slayton and Ivan Kinchloe. Two of my former squadron mates, Jim Carson and Lou Schalk were also there. It was great experience for me to have the opportunity to be able to talk to these men who day in and day out risked their lives testing aircraft that would eventually be used by relatively inexperienced pilots in the fighter squadrons.

I returned to Germany in October. In the spring of 1957, we were nearing the end of my tour in Germany. I decided to sell our reliable Plymouth station wagon and order a new Chevrolet station wagon to be picked up in New York. There was always a demand for good American cars in Germany. I also bought a new Volkswagen Karman Ghia with the idea of selling it at a profit when I reached the States.

My daydreaming ended abruptly at the sound of our bombs exploding somewhere near the prison. I felt the same euphoria that I felt every time our airplanes attacked. As always, I just wished the explosions would last longer and cause more damage.

# Chapter 18

Our bombing in and around Hanoi was becoming more frequent and more severe. Yet, my captors seemed to take the increased bombing effort in stride continuing to go about their daily routines and joining in the bucket brigades when the explosions caused fires. I wanted badly for our raids to bring them to their knees, but their nonchalant attitudes were ruining it for me.

It was seven weeks since I was shot down and this was a memorable day for me. Pigeye came into my cell to clip my beard and cut my hair. I wanted him to give me a burr haircut, but he refused. When he finished, he handed me a metal mirror and a razor and said, "Shave." He took me to Cell Number 8, locked me in and left.

I found a small piece of soap and tried to lather my face, but it was hopeless. I could not hold the soap. I carefully maneuvered the razor between my wrists and awkwardly attempted to shave. On the first stroke, I cut a gash about six inches long down the right side of my face. It started to bleed something awful. I tried to put cold water on my face to stop the bleeding, but it did not help.

Pigeye opened the metal framed window in the door and panicked when he saw the blood. He must have thought I was trying to commit suicide. He grabbed a towel and pressed it to my face to try to stop the bleeding. He rushed me back to my cell, took the razor and mirror and left hurriedly. He was probably supposed to be watching me and feared getting into trouble for leaving me alone with the razor.

It took two weeks for the cut to heal enough for Pigeye to attempt the shave idea again. This time I was more careful and managed to manipulate the razor by pressing my wrists tightly together with my palms facing inward. It was not a *Gillette* perfect shave but it was terrific for my face to feel clean. I had always taken pride in being clean shaven.

The unexpected bonus was getting a fresh set of underclothes and being allowed to clean myself. I got a new toothbrush and a small tube of toothpaste. "Much Bubbles – Good Taste – Made in Hanoi" it said on the tube. I also got a small bar of soap and a hand towel. I could not believe my good fortune.

I tried to see prisoners in the other cells as I walked back and forth to Cell Number 8 for my latrine visits. I loudly called out my name each time I passed by the other doors even though I knew I would get harshly slapped or beaten by Pigeye and Buff as punishment for breaking the rules. By bending at the waist to get a better angle, I could make out shadows under the cell doors but no bodies or faces. I desperately wanted to see another American face.

One afternoon in July, the guards installed a radio speaker in our cellblock hallway.  That evening at about dusk we were entertained by someone with an American accent reading some anti-war news articles over the radio. It was disgusting to me that one of my fellow American prisoners would stoop so low.  I could only surmise that whoever it was had succumbed to torture or the threat of intensified torture or even death.  The person doing the reading mispronounced some very common words and I had to wonder if it was their intentional way of letting the rest of us know they were being forced to speak.

Once the propagandizing was complete they played some good American music to complete the thirty-minute interlude.  The program left me feeling even more depressed as I sat staring at the four dirty walls of my stinking box of a cell.  I felt like I was at the bottom of a deep shaft totally without knowledge of the world around me.

The propaganda radio sessions would become a regular expectation of my daily routine as the days melted into weeks and months.  I learned to listen intently to filter out bits and pieces of useful news.  It was exasperating when I would pick up something that seemed credible and have nobody to discuss it with or pass it on to.

Alone in my cell, I drew heavily on my faith and prayed a lot.  I diligently worked at thinking about ways that I could survive this and still fulfill my responsibilities as a military officer.  I reflected back on my survival training and was determined to use all of my faculties to maintain my sanity. I paced the length of my seven-foot cell constantly, determined to keep my body in minimal functioning condition. It was hard considering the terrible diet, exposure to parasites and constant diarrhea, not to mention my badly abused body.

I dreamed constantly and reached a point that I craved sleep so that I could escape into my dreams. There were times that I got confused as to whether my dreams were in fact reality, since they would seem so real. I dreamed of being together again with my lovely wife Hazel, a dream that repeated often. I fondly remembered the time we went to the football game in Knoxville on our first date, my favorite reminiscence. I could smell the wonderful aroma of the Krispy Kreme donuts and taste their warm sugary sweetness as they melted in my mouth after each bite.

I took walks with my sons and swam in the beauty of their wonderful giggles as they played together in our various houses, which were also clear in my dream/memories. I found great pleasure in driving the Karman Ghia in my mind or remembering loading up the red and white Chevy station wagon for one move or another.

One morning I awoke clearly seeing a beautiful house in my consciousness that I had designed in my dream. I was totally energized by the idea of making a project of designing the house in great detail and building that house in my mind. I set about drawing the blue prints, although I had no training or knowledge how to go about it. Once I had the layout of rooms perfected, I started a list of materials I would need to construct the foundation and frame the walls.

I spent many months on my construction project and was rewarded with feelings of satisfaction each time I completed a bedroom or a bathroom or a kitchen. I took great joy in painting walls and window sills even though I was, in reality, not wild about painting. At times, I would become irritated when Pigeye or Buff would interrupt my home building to feed me or take me to dump my bucket. I knew that the house I was building was only in my imagination, but I made a commitment and promise to myself to go home one day and build that house for Hazel and my family.

Over the ensuing days, weeks and months, intermingled with my construction planning, I also immersed myself in reliving my life experiences. I renewed old relationships, recounted assignments and significant career events, and reveled in the joys of our family experiences. I exhaustively searched my memories for opportunities to identify "lessons learned", including positive and negative situations, upon which I could draw to help me survive this interminable hell.

I had fond memories of the places our assignments had taken us and the many experiences we shared. One year after arriving in Las Vegas, I was appointed as the

Director of Operations for the Weapons School and promoted to the rank of Major. I would supervise a broader range of flight operations and have the ability to delegate more responsibilities to others. The new role would quickly teach me, by necessity, how to focus on realistic expectations.

During my stay at Nellis AFB, I went to the Naval Weapons Center in California to learn how to use heat seeking missiles to shoot down enemy airplanes. On my return I was assigned the task of teaching three Taiwanese pilots how to use the weaponry. They returned home and shot down several Chinese airplanes over the Strait of Formosa. I would love to share that bit of knowledge with my Chinese interrogator who was so sensitive about Taiwan, I thought.

In March of 1960, we were advised that our Las Vegas duty would be ending, and true to our transient military lifestyle, it would soon be time to move on to our next adventure. I was advised that I had been selected to attend the Command and Staff College in Montgomery, Alabama. Major Allen Nelson, one of my colleagues in the Weapons School, was also selected to attend. Classes would begin the first of September and graduation would take place in June of 1961.

Attendance at the Command and Staff College would give me the opportunity to learn more about all divisions and segments of the Air Force and how the Air Force interacts with the Army, Navy, Coast Guard and civilian government agencies. Perhaps more importantly, I would be enlightened about how our government shares and exchanges military information with our allies.

We attended lectures featuring high ranking members of the military community and the federal government. During the first four months of our studies, military officers from allied countries addressed our classes. We exchanged secret classified information about how operations were conducted, comparing similarities and differences to our mutual benefit.

During May of 1961, I met with a career counselor to discuss my future in the Air Force. I had been thinking long and hard about where I wanted to go for my next assignment. From a military career perspective, I had trained for many years to be a fighter pilot and to prepare myself for war. However, timing and events over the years had precluded me from doing what I was trained to do, fly dog fights and drop bombs. I was starting to feel over trained and underutilized, but there was not an active war to fly off to. Thinking of my family, I felt a growing need to provide some stability.

Steve was about to finish ninth grade and had never attended the same school two years in a row. Hazel and I wanted him to go to a high school where he could remain for the entire three years. No one in either of our families had a college degree and we were determined to offer our sons the opportunity, even at the expense of furthering my career, if that ever proved to be the case. It was important to us for Steve to attend and graduate from one good high school.

The career counselor talked to me about a Pentagon staff assignment that would typically last four years and would fulfill our desires for stability during Steve's high school education. We decided that living in the nation's capital would be an interesting and educational opportunity and a far cry from the deep-south experience we were leaving. With Hazel's concurrence, I submitted an application to go to the Pentagon as a staff officer.

My class graduated on schedule in early June and we immediately packed and headed for Washington. On advice from friends, we found a house for rent in Falls Church, Virginia in a good neighborhood where Steve would be attending the highly recommended Jeb Stuart High School.

We settled into our new home and I reported to the Pentagon in my newly acquired used car. My first day was one of confusion. I did not know where I was allowed to park and I did not know where to sign in for duty. The sheer vastness of the Pentagon was overwhelming.

I finally figured out the parking and wandered around until I came across a young admiral who guided me to the Tactical Division of Operations. It was a little unsettling to learn that my office would be two floors below ground level.

I was soon greeted by my former Squadron

Commander at Foster AFB, now a Lieutenant Colonel, Richard Kenny. A short time later, Lieutenant Colonel Joe Kelsey came by to say hello. Joe and I were stationed together in Germany from 1949 to 1951. Both seemed to enjoy pointing out to me that in my new digs "they have to pump sunshine down a tube to get to you."

My new job as a Staff Officer at the Tactical Division of Air Force Operations was Program Element Monitor for the F-100 and F-104 aircraft fleet. In coordination with other elements of the Air Staff, I prepared a Five Year Force and Financial Plan based upon the projected number of F-100 and F-104 aircraft in use for each year. The budget was adjusted to account for the total number of aircraft decreased due to accidents or retirements. My estimates were based upon the number of pilots to be trained in those aircraft and the number of aircraft to be used for training purposes. My element was also responsible for projecting the amount of bombs, rockets, missiles and ammunition to be used annually for training purposes. I also assisted in the development of fighter training programs for the German and Japanese Air Forces that mirrored the USAF training programs.

On October 15, 1962, our Pentagon Air Force section was tasked to send a photo reconnaissance airplane over a suspected missile site in Cuba. An officer in our division was delegated as the Project Officer. A single RF-101 aircraft was sent over the suspected site at high speed. The film from the flight provided definitive proof that the

Soviet Union had moved medium range ballistic missiles into Cuba. This evidence brought about an international crisis between the United States and the Soviet Union.

The Air Force moved hundreds of fighter aircraft into bases in Florida and armed them with munitions. The strategic bombers went to their highest alert posture. All of this took place before President Kennedy informed the American people about the missiles.

Once President Kennedy went public with the announcement, our co-workers showed us the actual photos taken by the RF-101 photo plane. During the thirteen days that followed, schools all across America conducted drills teaching children to hide under their desks and cover their heads with their arms, a laughable exercise looking back.

Thanks to a naval blockade and tough stance by President Kennedy, the Russians ultimately caved and removed their armament to a collective sigh of relief heard around the world. Although it was not highly publicized, the U.S. agreed to remove its medium range missiles from Turkey and Italy. It was later learned that the Soviets had one squadron of high performance fighters in Cuba during the crisis and it remained there for one year.

In October of 1963, Steve received word that he had been accepted to attend Duke. We were overwhelmed with pride and excitement that our child would be attending such an outstanding university.

On November 22, 1963, our nation and the world went into shock upon learning that President John F. Kennedy was assassinated by Lee Harvey Oswald in Dallas, Texas. Immediately, the senior officers of the Air Force gathered in the Air Force Command Post and began to issue orders to the Combat Forces. All commercial phone lines in the Pentagon were closed except for the secure lines to the combat commands.

Nobody was allowed to make personal calls to their families. The Defense Department went into a war time posture. All civilian employees were sent home. Military members who did not have direct responsibilities were sent home at six that evening. In Dallas, Lyndon B. Johnson was sworn in as the 36th President of the Unites States at 3:38 PM.

Air Force One, the Presidential airplane, landed at Andrews AFB at 6:05 that evening with John F. Kennedy's body. The nation was in deep mourning. President Kennedy's remains were taken from the White House to the Capitol Rotunda and placed on the catafalque. More than 250,000 people, some waiting as long as three hours, filed by the President's casket. Hazel and I took our boys to the Capitol to see the throngs of mourners and as midnight approached, we returned home to Falls Church. It was an event that we would never forget.

One of the questions that came to mind as we watched the new President slowly and methodically assume his role as the Commander in Chief was, "What will happen in Vietnam?" Our nation had slowly been increasing the number of troops and military support to a government in South Vietnam that did not seem to understand its role. Our forces were supposed to be the advisors. However, more and more of the burden of fighting was being carried by American troops, our resources being used to support a regime that was corrupt and inept. Our government tried a variety of strategies from training and supporting ARVN divisions to establishing Special Forces camps to recruit the assistance of Montagnard mercenaries in an attempt to secure borders with Laos and Cambodia.

A most startling Vietnam event occurred in August of 1964 with the alleged attack by two North Vietnamese naval vessels on two U.S. Navy ships in the Gulf of Tonkin. The details of the sequence of events never clearly emerged but the story we got was that the U.S. Navy bombed targets in North Vietnam and one American Navy pilot was shot down and captured. The event raised the tensions between the U.S. and North Vietnam.

I was promoted to Lieutenant Colonel in the fall of 1964. I was also informed that I was the Air Staff Action Officer for the World Wide Tactical Gunnery Meet. The meet, a competition held to assess the effectiveness of pilots in fighter aircraft, would be held in October of 1964 at Nellis AFB, Nevada. I was surprised that the Air Force decided to hold the event considering all the resources that were being committed to the war in Vietnam.

I flew to Nellis to conduct a five-day planning conference for the Gunnery Meet. Representatives from the European and Pacific Commands and from Tactical Air Command in the United States gathered to write the rules for the competition. Afterwards, I met with representatives of the host base to work out the details of support agreements. I made two other short visits to Nellis prior to the actual competition.

I deeply regretted that while I was gone, Hazel had to go alone to take Steve to check into school and get settled in his dorm room at Duke University. Missing the opportunity to see him off to school was the most significant disappointment I could attribute to my military career, that is, until my airplane was shot down over Hanoi.

# Chapter 19

I had been in solitary confinement for 1004 consecutive days when suddenly, my cell door banged open and a much abused soldier was dragged into my cubicle. My new roommate was Colonel James Ellis Bean, an Air Force pilot.

During my period of captivity, I had seen only one American for about 10 seconds and even that was from a distance. I was excited to actually be with another American for the first time in so long, but I was immediately concerned about his beleaguered condition. He was badly burned.

I was surprised by the emotional impact of suddenly having the company of another American after so long. His presence produced an initial euphoria to know that someone else had endured worse treatment than I and survived. I felt guilty about this because I knew that I would not wish that on my worst enemy. However, it encouraged me somehow to know that there was someone else who would understand what I had lived through.

As I thought about sharing my cell, I had an immediate concern about allowing another person to observe my subhuman living conditions. I did not like the idea of presenting myself as an officer and looking and smelling as I did. I knew that the odor from living in my tiny cell with a nasty bucket for a latrine would attack anyone's personal hygiene consciousness. That thought raised another issue that I knew was silly as soon as I thought of it: What would it be like for someone to share my horrible black bucket? Perhaps the guards would find it in their hearts to provide an additional bucket.

As all of these thoughts raced through my mind, I realized my concerns needed to be concentrated on his physical condition. It was evident that he had been severely mistreated and abused. He was not initially capable of communicating. He only wanted to hold his head under a blanket and withdraw into himself. What had they done to him? I felt I knew.

At first, we were not able to do much talking because of his physical and mental condition. In addition, it had been so long since either of us had the chance to hold a normal conversation in English that we had to work on our communications skills.

I had no medicines or other means to treat his ailments any more than my own. All I could do was to talk to him and tell him that everything would be okay, especially since we now had each other to depend on.

Four months later, we were moved into a larger cell in a different cell block, still at Hoa Lo prison. We shared the cell with two other Air Force Colonels. We were not supposed to communicate with other prisoners. However, after over four years in captivity, I learned about the code that other prisoners had been using to tap out messages from cell to cell. It was simplistic, but very slow.

The code was developed by breaking our 25 letter alphabet (the letter "K" was not used) into five groups of letters in sequential order. We first tapped the number associated with the group, and then tapped the number designating the position of the letter in the group. A single tap referred to the first group, the letters "a" through "e". Three additional taps represented the letter "c", the third letter in the group. We found that we could send our messages not only by tapping, but by any means that we could generate a distinct sound, such as coughing and using a broom when sweeping.

In addition to "tapping", if we were lucky enough to find a sharp object, like a nail, we would scratch words on our eating utensils. This enabled us to pass on a message when these utensils were given to different prisoners.

In spite of these limitations, we were able to spread a lot of information. We learned that there were about two hundred American prisoners in the prison. There were ten other POW camps in the Hanoi area and prisoners were moved from one camp to the other.

Eventually, we were no longer tortured, but we were frequently slapped, kicked, and punched in the kidneys by the guards. It was over three years before we could have any communication with the outside world. On my third Christmas, the North Vietnamese softened their views slightly and we were allowed to write letters to our families. A short time later, I was excited to receive a package from my family containing toilet articles, candy and some underwear. I knew there must have been other items that were removed before the package got to me.

After some time, the Vietnamese allowed us to receive up to two packages per year. The guards rifled our packages and always knew the contents before we did. The food we received was limited but since all four of us had each lost thirty to thirty-five pounds since being captured, we happily shared it with one another. When our packages included letters and pictures from our families, the guards would allow us to keep them for a few days before cruelly taking them away. Our treatment was not "lenient and humane" as they proclaimed to the world.

In November of 1970, American Forces attempted to rescue some American prisoners from a camp near Sontay which was northwest of Hanoi. The attempt was not successful but it did prompt the North Vietnamese to transfer most of the American prisoners to one location in Hanoi, the Hanoi Hilton! We used our tapping system to establish contact with other prisoners and learned that there were more than five hundred now in our camp.

We senior officers were eventually placed in a group cell block that housed eight of us. It was there that I got to know Commander James Bond Stockdale.

He was on his second tour in Vietnam when, on

184

September 9, 1965, he was leading a mission over North Vietnam when his A4E aircraft was hit by flak. He was forced to eject into a village where he was brutally beaten by the locals. He was then taken to Hanoi and, while being moved around from camp to camp, was subjected to the same kind of torturous treatment I experienced. He had been kept in leg stocks for more than two years.

The North Vietnamese were so determined to break him that they tortured him to the point where he attempted suicide rather than break. They intended to parade him in front of journalists, but he cut his scalp with a razor and banged himself in the face with the infamous wood stool to prove that he had been mistreated. He cut his wrists to demonstrate that he would rather die than submit to his captors' demands that he admit that America was engaging in criminal acts against the North Vietnamese.

Like me, they offered him better living conditions and better treatment in exchange for being broken. Like me, he did not break. It was evident that he had continued to be abused even after more than four years in confinement.

The senior officers organized a Prisoner of War Wing composed of Air Force, Army, Navy, Marine Corps and allied prisoners from South Vietnam and Thailand. Even though some prisoners were located several hundred feet away, we managed to find ways to communicate with them. Our captors were constantly beating and abusing prisoners trying to discover how we communicated. They knew we had a system and were savage in their determination to discover and countermand it.

On two occasions, prisoners escaped and were re-captured. The escapees were brutally tortured and Captain Edwin Lee Atterberry died as a result of the torture. Several other prisoners were tortured as the Vietnamese attempted to learn who assisted or directed the escapes.

In May of 1971, approximately two hundred American prisoners were moved from the Hanoi Hilton to a new prison camp about 250 miles from Hanoi and only five miles from the Chinese border. That information came to us when one of those prisoners was brought back to Hanoi for medical treatment.

Twice a day, the Vietnamese had a propaganda program on the camp radio, at dusk and repeated again the next morning. It was the same garbage I had become accustomed to hearing. They tried to convince us that they were winning the war.

One morning, though, we were excited to hear in the program that the Vietnamese had been meeting with an American delegation in Paris for many months seeking a way to end the war. We knew that we would not get accurate reports about how the talks proceeded, but were just elated to learn that talks were taking place.

We discovered that some of our prisoners made statements to visiting "peace delegations" that sounded favorable to the Vietnamese about our treatment and care as prisoners. We did not know whether the Americans made the statements voluntarily or were coerced through torture to make the statements. Accordingly, we did not make judgments about the contents of their statements but we did judge them if they accepted favorable treatment as a result.

Some prisoners met with anti-war groups and were rewarded with food and beverages. Some of them then encouraged the younger officers to accept favorable treatment. Those actions were in violation of the Code of Conduct and our senior officer ordered the prisoners to cease those actions and obey the Code. Our senior officer ordered them to resist the propaganda programs of the North Vietnamese.

The longer the war dragged on, more and more prisoners felt that they had been abandoned by their government. It became increasingly difficult to maintain prisoner moral when they saw American citizens visit and heard that Americans were protesting against their own country. Our senior officer also ordered everyone to continue to resist the Vietnamese and not to accept an early release which would reflect that they were in agreement with the protestors. Twelve prisoners did accept early releases in defiance of that order.

# Chapter 20

We were proud to hear on the radio one morning that the U.S. had successfully landed two men on the moon. I wondered how in the world our country could accomplish such a feat without being able to reach diplomatic solutions here on earth. Once in a while we would hear some American music, but most of the time all we got was propaganda.

One day in April of 1972, we heard bombs exploding in the distance and recognized that it was a B-52 bombing raid. I imagined hearing the *Star Spangled Banner* playing in the background to celebrate the occasion. The next day the radio broadcast included a report about the bombing of Hai Phong Harbor. That was encouraging news for us! In an effort to generate sympathy from us, the North Vietnamese dragged some of us through a Hanoi Museum in July of 1972 to see some of the bomb casings and other munitions dropped by the bombers.

We sensed that something positive was happening when the Vietnamese gave us physical examinations including chest x-rays in August. They "invited" us to write a statement detailing the injuries the Vietnamese had inflicted on us, making it clear that only positive comments would be accepted. Torture had virtually ceased at that time except for the most flagrant violations of camp regulations.

In October the political officer came into our compound and announced that the war would end soon. You could almost feel the energizing effect through the walls of the compound. But, in early November, only weeks later, the camp radio announced that the North Vietnamese had recalled their delegation from the Paris Peace Talks. Our morale roller coaster kept going up and down.

The camp guards gave each one of our group a notebook and a pencil in late November and informed us that they were to be used for study purposes. They told us that the notebooks were for academic use only, "no politics." They collected the notebooks every few days to see what the "blackest of criminals" had written. Surprisingly, they distributed Bibles for us to read and study for one week. We knew something had to be happening somewhere to influence our captors' sudden generosity.

On December 18, 1972, just after sundown, we heard the unmistakable sound of bomb blasts around Hanoi. The number of explosions and the firing of SAMs told us that Hanoi was being attacked by B-52 bombers. The earth shook and the camp lights went out immediately. We rushed to the window openings to watch the activity and to see the huge fireballs.

A cheer erupted from within the prison walls so loud and boisterous it almost drowned out the rumble of two-thousand pound bombs exploding. It was a testament to the American spirit that had been silenced within these walls for the more than five years of my captivity. As our excitement escalated and our cheers for the bomber crews grew louder, North Vietnamese guards charged into the compound armed with fixed bayonets and roughly forced us to get under the wooden beds.

The soldiers silently withdrew when they were satisfied that they had sufficiently subdued all of the prisoners. As soon as they were gone, we were immediately at the windows again watching the fires burning near the camp. The massive rumbling and concussive explosions pounded our ears and sent joy to our hearts.

One fantastic effect from B-52 raids is the silence before and after. They soar at such great altitude that you have no idea airplanes are above you until the sudden and unexpected panorama of fire and noise that rains from the sky. Although we did not know it then, one hundred twenty-nine B-52's took part in the all night raid. Much to our disappointment, the bombing ended at sunrise.

Like entertainment scheduled for our pleasure, the bombers returned the next night, Tuesday, December 19 and every night except Christmas through the end of the month. The bombing suddenly ceased at midnight on December 29. We waited anxiously for some information. Finally, the camp radio announced that the North Vietnamese delegation had returned to Paris to resume peace talks.

# Chapter 21

On January 29, 1973, the Vietnamese gathered twenty-nine of us senior officer prisoners into the courtyard and provided us a copy of the Peace Agreement. These wonderful pages made it official that our release was imminent. It was the first opportunity I had to put faces together with names I had subversively exchanged communication with for so long.

According to the protocol, the sick or wounded POW's would be the first to be released. However, the Vietnamese would designate the sick and wounded instead of allowing our officers to make the selections.

We, the senior officers, decided that we would leave the prison in a military formation with our heads held high. The senior officer for each group would give the commands and insure that every soldier acted in a military manner during the release proceedings. If any of our fellow prisoners could not walk, we, not the Vietnamese, would carry them.

Following the release of the sick and wounded, the sequence would be first-in, first-out basis according to date of capture. We required that each POW know the name and the capture date of the person ahead of him. If the Vietnamese did not allow us to follow the sequence, then everything would come to a standstill. We would not knowingly leave anyone behind.

According to the protocol, the first group of POW's would be released on Monday, February 12, 1973. The second group would be released fourteen days later, the third group would be released fourteen days after the second group, and the last group would be released fourteen days after the third group. Each group would total about one hundred and fifty POW's.

In preparation for our release, the North Vietnamese issued each POW a pair of dark trousers, a light colored shirt, a pair of black shoes and a light windbreaker. We were given a small bag for any personal belongings that we wanted to take such as letters or photographs and the odd memorabilia like toiletries received in packages from home.

Navy Commander James B. Stockdale was the senior officer and in command of the first group based on his capture date of Thursday, September 9, 1965. The soldier who would lead the first group out of the Hanoi Hilton would be Everett Alvarez who was captured on Wednesday, August 5, 1964. He was finally being released eight and one-half years after his capture.

The Vietnamese allowed us to form up and watch the first company sized group of prisoners as they marched out of the prison. Although I personally had only lived with eight other people during my captivity, a lasting bond was formed among all of us who shared the Hanoi Hilton experience. It was an amazingly emotional moment for those marching as well as those watching. I would lead the second group to be released based on my date of capture, Friday, May 12, 1967. I was informed by camp officers that they were going to make a special release of eighteen POW's in honor of Secretary of State Henry Kissinger who was at Gia Lam Airport in Hanoi. The men the North Vietnamese selected would be taken out of the first-in, first-out sequence so I ordered the men not to leave the prison. I advised the camp officials that the men could not leave unless I was told to release them by an American official.

Those men were not collaborators but they had not caused the Vietnamese any trouble and they were being rewarded for it. At noon an Air Force Lieutenant Colonel came into the camp to talk to me. He confirmed that the Secretary was in fact waiting for the men to arrive. I released the group and instructed them to put on their clothing and march out of the camp. One of the men who did not want to be stigmatized by the early release rushed back to ask if he could wait for me at Clark AFB in the Philippines. I told him absolutely not and instructed him to "get his butt on that airplane."

The exceptional release ordered by the Secretary caused the release of my group to be delayed six days. The Vietnamese explained to me that we were delayed because the U.S. was not complying with the agreement.

We were released on Sunday, March 4, 1973. Since I had caused trouble for the Vietnamese, they held me until the last bus going to the airport. I resumed my proper position in the release sequence after arrival at the airport. My group included two noncommissioned officers from the Thailand Air Force. Since they understood the Vietnamese language, they were able to provide us with invaluable intelligence information about activities happening within the prison camp. For security reasons, upon arrival at Clark AFB, they were to be separately and discreetly taken to the base hospital for special treatment and to receive physical examinations.

While we were en route to Clark, the Public Information Officer asked if I would like to address the reception upon arrival. It was a bit overwhelming when we were greeted by more than one thousand military family members and friends. I thanked the President and everyone who made it possible for us to be free men again. I pointed out that there were still many prisoners in North Vietnam and we should refrain from doing or saying anything that would delay their release. I explained that our average time as prisoners was five years and now that the nightmare was ending, we could begin to rebuild our lives.

We were fed a sumptuous meal of steak and eggs before we began our processing. Late on that first evening, I invited anyone in our group who was interested to meet in the chapel for a worship and thanksgiving service. Many of us largely attributed our survival to our religious beliefs.

The Department of Defense had developed a magnificent plan to care for us and our families as we returned to a "normal" lifestyle. "Operation Homecoming" was the foundation of the rebuilding process.

The plan prescribed that I would receive a letter written by my family telling me about the significant events that occurred in my family while I was incarcerated. I feel sure it was intended as a bridge to help us to overcome any possible awkward or traumatic moments that could occur on initial contact after so long. It was a necessary exercise before the POW's made actual face-to-face contact with our families.

I was informed that, following an all-important initial telephone call with my family, I would have a physical and dental checkup, followed by a fitting for a new uniform. I would ultimately be flown to a military hospital near my home and be reunited with my family. While at the hospital, I would undergo a thorough physical examination and treatment as necessary. We had not had much medical treatment during our incarceration, even those of us who were severely injured during the events leading up to our capture. We all had intestinal problems caused by parasites. In addition to health care, the hospitalization was required to give us some time to rest and to adjust to a new situation and a new lifestyle.

Afterwards, I would undergo extensive intelligence debriefing. Eventually, personnel representatives would meet with me to determine whether I wanted to remain in service.

Once we completed the initial processing, I was finally allowed to call my family. It was an emotional conversation for all of us. I could not believe that I was finally speaking with my family as I had dreamed of doing all those long days and nights during captivity. Hearing Hazel's voice on the other end of the line was like speaking to an angel in heaven. It did not seem like she had changed at all. My boys had obviously matured and I felt certain living through those years of my absence had forced them to grow up much too fast.

This was a doubly special day for me since it was not only my first day of freedom in 2,124 days, but also Steve's twenty-seventh birthday and I could wish him Happy Birthday in person. The combination of pride and the sense of urgency to see them and hold them overwhelmed me. I assured them that I was well and that I would return to the United States as soon as possible.

While waiting for completion of the preliminary examination in the Clark hospital, one of my friends from my time in the Pentagon came into my room and welcomed me home. He mentioned that "great things have happened to you while you were in prison." Later, a Navy Admiral whom I did not know came in and congratulated me. I was confused by these comments.

A while later, I was asked to come into a room for a fitting of my new uniform. It was slightly large for me and already had my service ribbons and insignia on it. It was well past midnight when I finally went to bed. I am not certain that some of the younger officers went to bed at all that night. It was a time of jubilation for all of us.

The day following our release, over one hundred more prisoners captured in South Vietnam and Laos were flown in from Hanoi. The group consisted of U.S. military personnel and U.S. civilian employees. Also in the group were two German nurses, one male and one female. Some of the group had been prisoners for three years and they were kept in jungle cages as they moved from the south to the north. I assumed responsibility for the group as they were processed through the Reception Center.

When my group finished their processing, I was advised that it was time to leave for the States. Air Force Colonel Layton McDonald was appointed to accompany me to the hospital at Andrews AFB, Maryland. I was mentally and physically exhausted. There were beds on the aircraft and the doctors advised me to sleep during the flight to Hawaii. There were about twenty-five other former POW's on the plane. We stopped in Hawaii to refuel before flying on to Andrews.

When we landed in Hawaii, we were greeted by hundreds of military families even though it was two o'clock in the morning. Landing on the American tarmac brought home the sensational realization that after almost six years in Hanoi, I was finally and truly free. Those North Vietnamese bastards could never touch, control or harm me again. Boots Blesse, my friend and flight leader when I was shot down and captured on May 12, 1967, was there to greet me. We had a lot to talk about.

# Chapter 22

The plane departed at about six in the morning for another eight hour flight to Andrews AFB. I was told that Hazel, Steve, Tony, Dale, my granddaughter Leslie, my grandson Nathan, my mother Allie and my sister Opal would be there to greet me. When the plane arrived, I looked out the door and saw hundreds of people there to welcome us home. But I did not initially see my family.

I was greeted by my friend, General Daniel "Chappie" James. I thanked everyone there for their loyalty and their concern and support. I, again, thanked the President for his actions. Then I looked to my left to see Hazel sprinting to greet me. The rest of the family walked slowly behind her wanting to allow us those precious first moments to reunite. Once we released each other from that emotional embrace, the others trotted over to greet me with huge smiles on their faces. It was, without a doubt, the happiest day of my life.

After a few moments together, we walked over to shake hands with our greeters. Some were our former neighbors and the others were friends and well-wishers. I thanked them for remembering us during the long years of incarceration.

We were escorted over to the staff cars that would take us to the mess hall for an evening meal. The youngest member of our family, Nathan, slept contentedly in his bassinet on the table. I do not remember what we ate for dinner but I do remember the heavenly, clean and innocent baby smells that reminded me just how much of life I had missed. I remember that we did a lot of talking and that little Leslie's meal was crackers.

It seemed so unreal for me to be with my family after so many, many long years of separation. But here I was among my loved ones, forty-nine years old and the grandfather of two beautiful grandchildren.

We were allowed to visit for two days before I started taking extensive physical examinations and meeting with the intelligence debriefing team. All of the family except Hazel left to go home.

During my stay in the hospital, members of Jim Jefferson's family came to visit. I spent a lot of time with them sharing what I knew of his status, including my belief that he was not killed when the plane crashed. While it left many of their questions unanswered, they very much appreciated the information that I was able to provide.

When things slowed down a bit, we contacted our friends who were still living in the Washington area and invited them to come to the base to visit us. It was an opportunity for us to thank them personally for their love and support of Hazel during the years I was away in

Vietnam.

We were invited to have dinner with Major General John Roberts and his wife Fern. General Roberts was the Director of Military Personnel at that time. He later rose to the four star level. We flew with the same squadron in Neubiberg, Germany in 1949. During the evening, I related the incident to him about the two Senior Officers coming into my room at Clark AFB and inferring that I had been promoted while I was in prison. He was troubled by the story since the promotion process and the results are known by only a few people. He assured me that he would discuss the matter with his superior officer, General Robert Dixon, as quickly as possible.

My two much needed weeks in the hospital passed quickly and I was given a ninety-day rehabilitation leave. A welcome home committee from Winston-Salem flew in a private airplane to Washington to bring Hazel and me home. Tony and one of his friends, Susan Fleming, were on the airplane to greet us.

There was a terrific welcoming crowd at the Smith-Reynolds Airport even though it was raining and windy. The weather did not dampen the spirits of the crowd. One of my POW friends, David Hatcher, who was released in the first group, was there to offer a prayer for us and our country. I was humbled by the welcome home ceremony. I was not a hero and did not seek adulation. I considered myself to be a military man whose duty placed me in difficult circumstances and by the grace of God, I was able to survive.

On the ride from the airport to our apartment, I saw a huge sign across the road that read:

*"Welcome Home Colonel Gaddis - We Prayed For You"*

Over the next several weeks, I felt the immense love and patriotism that Americans have for their country and for those who serve in the Armed Forces.

# Chapter 23

Six years had passed since Hazel and I said goodbye to one another and we had so very much to talk about. Many incredible things had happened in our lives and we sat snuggled together for hours sharing our stories and the stories of our families, children and grandchildren.

While a POW, our foremost concern was about our immediate families. How had they handled the agony of the long separation? The uncertainty of my status for the first three years was a burden for all of them. As they faced and dealt with each situation, they asked themselves the question, "What would Dad have us do; and if we did it would it cause him embarrassment or retribution?" Hazel's recounting of those years for them revealed that they had handled themselves with great dignity. I was extremely proud of every one "of them.

Hazel told me about the plight of our country while I was away. I was incredulous when she told me about the assassinations of Martin Luther King and Bobby Kennedy, the race riots and the anti-war demonstrations. It almost sounded like my country was at war at home during those turbulent years.

Hazel told me that it was only through my first letter to

her that the Air Force learned that I was still alive. She contacted the Air Force Intelligence and advised them that she had received a letter from me. After questioning her about the wording and information in the letter to validate that I had actually written it, she was allowed to notify my family of my status. This approval was necessary because the Department of Defense asked the families of men captured in Vietnam not to publicize the fact that their loved ones were being held in North Vietnam.

Hazel explained to me that when this restriction was initiated in 1969, the U.S. and the North Vietnamese were meeting in Paris to attempt to negotiate an end to the war. If personal information on the prisoners was released to the news media, unscrupulous people could try to exploit the situation and possibly cause the talks to break off.

The policy was not popular with the families who were growing weary with the never-ending negotiations. Many did not believe that our government and the North Vietnamese were serious about ending the war. The wives and families wanted the war to end quickly.

She shared with me how she and two other wives of POW's had met with the Mayor of Winston-Salem and Congressman Wilmer Mizelle of North Carolina and briefed them on the plight of the POW's and solicited their support. Hazel visited the state capital, Raleigh, and talked to many members of the legislative assembly. While in Raleigh they planted a tree adjacent to the Legislative Building and dedicated it to the POW's and

MIA's.

She also visited with Senator John Duncan of Tennessee. She and her group also raised the issue of men who were missing in action (MIA) and asked the legislators to pursue grants for financial relief for their families.

In late 1969, a group of the wives organized the National League of Families of POW's and MIA's. They publicized the fact that the men were not treated in accordance with the Geneva Convention. They were not being allowed to write to their families nor were they being allowed to receive letters and packages from their families.

Hazel agreed to be the North Carolina coordinator for the League that represented eighty North Carolina families who had members being held as prisoners, were listed as missing in action or were killed in Southeast Asia. She spent many hours contacting and counseling with family members.

Some of the wives were young and inexperienced while others were the parents of young men and they had not dealt with military matters before. There were family relationship problems, cases of infidelity and misspending of servicemen's pay. Hazel was a listener, a counselor and a confidant.

She encouraged and went with many of the families to Washington to attend family briefings. The League persuaded the Department of Defense to have regular meetings with the families to discuss important matters. They convinced the State Department to keep them briefed on the Paris negotiations.

A highly successful project was "No Greater Love". Carol Bates Brown was the National Chairman of the POW/MIA Bracelet Campaign for VIVA (Voices In Vital America), the Los Angeles based student organization that produced and distributed the bracelets during the Vietnam War. Entertainers Bob Hope and Martha Raye served with her as honorary co-chairmen. The idea for the bracelets was started by Brown and fellow college student, Kay Hunter to remember American prisoners of war suffering in captivity in Southeast Asia.

Hazel ordered and sold hundreds of the bracelets with my name on them and some with other POW names on them. It allowed the wearer to empathize with the person whose name was on the bracelet while showing support for the family. Hazel socked the money away to show me when I returned home, which she never doubted I would do. When we returned home from Andrews AFB hospital, I helped Hazel count the money from the sale of the bracelets and it was over $800. Together we sent it to *No Greater Love* to add to the $1,000 she had already submitted in my name.

I received over five hundred letters from bracelet wearers. They were so happy to know that I survived the ordeal in North Vietnam. One letter described a scene when the sender was in the delivery room and the doctor asked her to remove the bracelet. She told him the story of the bracelet and he permitted her to keep it on during her delivery. Another writer told me that my bracelet was buried with her mother at her mother's request. I received many telephone calls from people who wore my bracelets. Even now I continue to receive letters from the children of the person who wore my bracelet. There is still a very special bond that exists among us.

Perhaps the most profound project that the National League of Families was involved in was a letter writing campaign to the North Vietnamese negotiators in Paris. The various State Coordinators were asked to have Americans write a letter criticizing the Vietnamese government for not allowing the prisoners to write to their families or to receive packages of food and clothing from them. With assistance from Bill East, a reporter from the Winston-Salem Journal & Sentinal, the writing program produced many hundreds of letters. Hazel's sister conducted a similar campaign in Knoxville. So many letters arrived at the Vietnamese Embassy in Paris that the authorities finally refused to accept any more.

Once the Vietnamese allowed prisoners to receive packages, the State Department and the Air Force coordinated the determination of the allowable items as well as the weight and size of each package and provided this information to the families. We never knew for sure what caused the North Vietnamese to change their position and allow prisoners to receive letters and packages from home, but we felt certain that the letter writing campaign could be at least partially credited.

Hazel was patient and wonderful as she tried to fill in the blanks for me of the things that happened during my absence. So much had transpired that I imagined she was growing weary of my questions and ignorance of the simplest of things. Fortunately, the Air Force designed a two-week program to be conducted by the Air University at Maxwell Air Force Base covering the significant events from 1965 until 1973 to help us to bridge the information gap we experienced while we were in prison. Hazel and I traveled to Montgomery and attended and found it to be most helpful.

That two week period reviewing the past helped us to focus on our future and to openly discuss whether we wanted to retire or remain in the service. Hazel had managed our finances wonderfully in my absence. When I arrived in Vietnam in 1966, I allocated all of my pay and allowances except three hundred dollars monthly to Hazel. I had also left her a power of attorney to sell our house in Victoria, Texas.

Hazel had traded our 1966 Pontiac Tempest for a new Buick LaSabre in 1972 and paid it off in one year. She also invested each month in a Government Savings Program for military personnel serving in combat and had managed to grow that account to more than fifty-three thousand dollars by the time I returned home. Her efforts would enable us to retire if that was what we chose to do.

I had an itch to fly again and that would require that I remain in the Air Force. In spite of what both Hazel and I had been through, we both still seemed too young to be contemplating retirement. It was a decision we would need to make mutually and I needed to know that it was right for Hazel before we made a commitment. After much thought and discussion, Hazel finally said to me "if you want to stay in the Air Force a while longer, I will be there for you."

# Chapter 24

In the weeks that followed, we needed to respond to telephone calls and letters from people, some of whom we knew personally and others casually. Even though the war was not especially popular with the nation, most Americans were showing their respect and admiration for those of us who suffered through long years of confinement and family separation.

We accepted invitations to speak and visit many churches, schools and civic clubs to share our stories. It was stressful to meet and talk with families of the men who were killed in action or still missing in action. We hoped that speaking with a survivor and wife who have lived through the terrible ordeal of separation would somehow help families who continued to suffer. At least, we provided them with firsthand information.

During that time, the Air Force informed me that it had organized a special requalification course at Randolph AFB for those POW's who wanted to remain in active service and fly again. It would not be a structured program but rather allow each of us to progress at our own pace. I would have sixty days to complete the course. I was nearly fifty years old, my reflexes were still fairly good and I wanted to requalify in jets. I requested to arrive at Randolph AFB about the middle of July 1973.

When we prisoners returned home from Vietnam, many companies and individuals offered us gifts and/or special discount prices on goods and services. The Department of Defense asked us to decline the offers until it could determine whether or not those companies had contracts with the government or were seeking to do business with the federal government. Shortly thereafter, the D.O.D. published a list of companies from whom we could accept gifts, so I accepted a five hundred dollar voucher from the Clothing Manufacturers of America and the use of a Ford Mustang for one year. Ford Motor Company agreed to sell me the car after one year at a special discount price. I went to a Ford dealer in Winston-Salem and selected a light blue Mustang. I declined many other offers.

We drove from Winston-Salem to San Antonio in our new Mustang, stopping in Memphis to see family. We rented an apartment in San Antonio, near Randolph where I would start my requalification training in jets.

The training went smoothly and my qualification was followed by a dousing of champagne. After the celebration, Lieutenant General William McBride, Commander of Air Training Command, invited me to his office to discuss the retraining program. General McBride was a very warm and friendly person. I remembered his being in the Pentagon as the Special

Assistant to the Secretary of the Air Force. I told him that I was impressed with the organizational planning and the personnel selected to do the training. I shared with him that I felt that it was a first class operation and I was thankful that the Air Force was giving us an opportunity to fly again.

He then redirected the conversation to ask me what I wanted to do after I finished my requalification. I was not at all bashful. I said I would like to go back to Arizona to command Williams Air Force Base where I had received my training as a fighter pilot and the location of the school I thought of as my "alma mater." I did not mention any other alternatives. He replied that he would talk with me later.

Two weeks later, General McBride summoned me to his office again. He informed me that the current Commander at Williams had been there three years and would be moving early the following year. He wanted me to go to Williams after I completed my training to serve as the Deputy Commander for a few months. I thanked him profusely for the opportunity to get that experience.

In less than sixty days, I completed approximately fifty hours and was fully requalified for flying jets. It was time to move on to my next assignment. We arrived at the base on September 1, 1974. A couple of days later we were assigned a house on the base.

Once we were moved in and settled I reported in with the base commander, Colonel Warren Moore. He welcomed me and introduced me to his senior staff. It was an awkward moment. I was senior to all of the Colonels on the base. I expressed my appreciation to the staff and let them know that I was there to learn how to command and I wanted to learn from them. I told them I would be coming to their offices in the next new few days to visit with them.

Tony enrolled at Chandler High School to complete his senior year. He signed up for the cross country running team. Soon after he started training for the team I was called back from flying a mission and asked to proceed to the base hospital to meet Hazel. There was a problem with Tony. We had noticed that Tony sweated profusely when he exercised but attributed it to the Phoenix climate.

When I arrived at the hospital, the doctors advised us that Tony's left kidney was five times its normal size and it was infected. He needed an immediate operation to remove the kidney. He would have to be transferred to Mesa Hospital since the base hospital did not have a surgical team to perform the surgery.

After the surgery, the team of doctors advised us that full recovery would take several weeks. Tony slowly regained his strength and we were finally able to take him home but we had to rush him back to the hospital when he developed a staphylococcus infection. After a few more days of treatment the doctors were able to cure the infection and we were relieved to be able to take him home once again.

I continued to feel confused about the subject of my promotion that had inappropriately surfaced on my release from prison. Major General John Roberts, Director of Military Personnel for the Air Force had discussed the matter with the Deputy Chief of Personnel, and I had received an eyes only letter from General Dixon before I left Randolph AFB in San Antonio. The letter informed me that the Air Force was negligent in completing my records when I was declared Missing in Action. It also informed me that the two officers responsible for completing my records, both now Major Generals would be directed to render an Effectiveness Report on my performance while at Cam Ranh Bay. It said I would be promoted on the next promotion list after he received their reports.

On January 25, 1974, I received a call from General McBride. It certainly got my attention when he said, "This is General McBride and I don't normally call at 5:00AM unless you are in trouble! But you are not in trouble! I have some good news for you. As of 8:00AM eastern standard time, you were promoted to Brigadier General. Now go back to bed and get some sleep." I replied, "Thank you, Sir!" And, no, we did not go back to sleep.

When I arrived at my office at 9:00AM, Colonel Moore, Base Commandeer, called me to his office and asked if I received a call this morning from General McBride. I told him that I had talked to the General earlier. He said, "He also called me." I asked if he had been promoted and he responded, "Yes!" Warren and I laughed and congratulated one another. Now what would happen to us?

A couple of hours later I received another call from General McBride informing me that as of noon that day, I would be the Commander of Williams AFB and Colonel Moore would be moving immediately to Colorado to be the Commander of Air Force Technical Training Command. I met with the staff and shared the news with them.

It was a rapid transition as Hazel and I moved into the Commander's Quarters. It was a most rewarding and humbling experience to command the base from which I was graduated thirty years earlier. I looked forward to being with a highly professional group of instructors each day and an equally eager group of students.

# Chapter 25

Soon after I assumed my new duties, I received notification from the Air Force Surgeon General that the Air Force School of Aviation Medicine at Brooks AFB, Texas, was engaged in a study of the long-term effects of incarceration of Prisoners of War. It was similar to what the Navy had been doing with POW's since World War II. I was invited to be a part of the study. I went to the school for a series of physical and psychological examinations. During a treadmill test, the doctors determined that I apparently had a blockage in my heart arteries. I was asked to return to the school in a couple of weeks and be prepared to undergo a cardiac catheterization to determine the extent of the blockage.

I returned to the school in late May and spent two days in the hospital. After the tests were completed, I was told that I would be contacted after the results were thoroughly reviewed and was released to go back to Williams. The instructor pilot who flew with me to Randolph gently suggested that I probably should not fly the airplane back. I agreed and slowly got into the back seat and let the ground crew strap me in.

About a week later, I received a call from General

McBride to tell me the doctors found sufficient blockage in my arteries to permanently ground me from flying as a pilot. It came as a shock to me. Now after being a commander for only four months, I could not remain in that position and would have to be reassigned. Nonetheless, I felt extremely honored to have had the privilege of commanding the Air Force's largest pilot training base even for a short time.

Tony graduated high school in May of 1974. The removal of his kidney denied him the dream of going to the Air Force Academy. He was not sure where he wanted to go to college and we encouraged him to take his time making his life decisions knowing he could rely on us to be there for him.

Even though I had learned that I was to be promoted back in January, it was June 1, 1974 before I was authorized to pin on my new rank. We invited Steve, Dale and the grandchildren to fly out and be with us on that special day. Hazel, Steve and Tony pinned on the stars.

The latter part of May 1974, my friend, Major General John Roberts, called to inform me that I was going to be transferred to Air Force Headquarters in Washington, DC. I was directed to report to the Pentagon as the Deputy Director for Air Force Operations not later than July 15th. As was the time-honored tradition, the Training Wing held a Change of Command Ceremony as I relinquished command to Colonel Earl Brown, the first African-

American to hold such a position. He was not only my close friend, but also an officer and a gentleman.

Hazel and I traveled to Washington and located a house in Arlington that suited our needs. But the price was $53,000. We were suffering from sticker shock. We bought it and wondered if we would ever get our money back.

My new assignment brought with it onerous responsibilities and long work hours. The situation in Southeast Asia was getting worse instead of better. Our bombers were still dropping bombs in South Vietnam. The Air Force was reducing its aircraft fleet and releasing many of its most experienced personnel. While the nuclear strike forces remained much the same, the tactical forces were being downsized.

Flying hours were being reduced and flight crews were training in flight simulators. Finally, in April of 1975, Congress cut off all funds for the bombing in South Vietnam. That would lead to an end of the longest war in our history, from 1961 until 1975. Over fifty-seven thousand Americans lost their lives, more than three-hundred thousand were wounded and over twenty-five hundred men were missing in action. And the U.S. fell far short of achieving any significant goals in South Vietnam. Many Americans were furious with the government for its handling of the Vietnam War, especially in the dishonorable way it ended.

President Nixon stood fast behind his threats to bomb

North Vietnam if they did not abide by the Paris Peace Agreement. The North Vietnamese feared Nixon and believed he would follow through on his threats. However, when the President was impeached as a result of the Watergate break-in scandal and President Ford took office, the North Vietnamese had renewed confidence in their ability to invade South Vietnam without the threatened American intervention.

My duties were almost 24 hour per day. The Air Force installed a Red Telephone in my bedroom and I was required to answer it by the third ring. I had to stay in close contact with the Air Force Command Post. It was stressful, but that was part of my job. I was allowed to be off duty periodically and to take a leave occasionally. When a crisis arose, I went with the Air Force Deputy for Operations and Plans to the Air Force Command Center. During those international crises, I would often stay in the Pentagon for days at a time. Hazel would bring me clean clothes and some home-cooked food.

I was in the Command Center while our forces evacuated the diplomatic staff from the U.S. Embassy in Phnom-Penh, Cambodia and two weeks later, while U.S. Marines recaptured the Mayaguez from terrorists in the Gulf of Thailand.

The North Vietnamese invasion of South Vietnam was swift and methodical, like a wave of terror that washed down the country from north to south. Ambassador Graham Martin desperately wanted to evacuate the South

Vietnamese citizens working in the embassy and their families along with South Vietnamese loyalists to the Americans. But, the American Congress refused to allot additional funding to facilitate the massive evacuation. Ambassador Martin continually refused to get on a helicopter to evacuate.

I was in the Pentagon Command Center while our forces evacuated the American diplomatic staff from the U.S. Embassy. On the morning of April 30, 1975, I received instructions as a Presidential Order to personally call Ambassador Martin directly and inform him that "President Ford said to get your butt on the next helicopter coming out of Saigon." He was evacuated by helicopter from the roof of the U.S. Embassy that morning as Communist forces overran the city.

I knew that after we were released from captivity, Max had reunited with his family in Saigon. I took the liberty of inquiring with our intelligence officers about whether Max had gotten out before our final evacuation of Saigon and learned that Ross Perot had sent his team to fly Max and his family to America.

In the aftermath of the U.S. withdrawal from Vietnam, emotions among Americans were all over the place. War protestors who vehemently opposed the war celebrated their final victory. People who served in the war and their families mourned the waste of their comrades, relatives and their own sacrifices, at the same time feeling relief that it was finally over. People like me who had been

Prisoners of War, while happy that no other Americans would be taken prisoner in that forsaken place, were in a state of shock and disbelief.

# Chapter 26

In May of 1976, I submitted my request for retirement to the Chief of Staff, General David C. Jones. He reluctantly approved it. On June 1, 1976, I retired from the Air Force with thirty years and three months of service and 4300 hours of flying time. I left the Air Force knowing that it had men of utmost dedication and outstanding character to lead it in times of peace and times of war. It had been an honor for me to serve my country.

General Jones held my retirement ceremony in his office. The Honorable John Lucas, Secretary of the Air Force, all of the Air Force General Officers in the Pentagon and my staff were invited to attend and say goodbye to Hazel and me. General Jones presented me with a Certificate of Retirement and to Hazel he gave a Certificate of Appreciation for her unselfish, faithful and devoted service to the Air Force. It was an emotional experience for both of us. We were indeed honored to have had the opportunity to serve our nation through some very difficult and trying times. Now the mantle of my responsibilities would pass on to the warriors of a new generation.

*Lest He Never Be Forgotten*
*In Memoriam*

*Lieutenant Colonel James Milton Jefferson was apparently killed during the ejection, while parachuting or immediately after he landed. His remains were recovered and identified by DNA process at the Hanoi crash site on June 5, 2000, thirty-three years after the bailout. He was presumed to have died on May 12, 1967.*

*Vietnam Memorial Wall, Panel 19E, Row 96*

# About The Author

Bill Norris lives in Florida with his wife, Sheila, and four cats. He is an entrepreneur who has created businesses with operations in most states in the U.S., across Canada, and in Mexico. Bill is a veteran of the Vietnam War. *Dagger Four Is OK, Brig. Gen. Norman Gaddis POW Memoir*, is Bill's recently completed second book. His first book, *Flying Into The Storm* released in 2014, tells of his experiences as an air mobile infantry soldier in 1968 flying numerous helicopter combat assault missions and living the life of a grunt soldier, boots on the ground. It has been called Stephen Crane's *Red Badge of Courage* for Vietnam.

Bill holds a Bachelor of Arts in Business Administration from Lenoir Rhyne College (now University) in his hometown of Hickory, North Carolina. Although not a pilot in the war, he developed a love for flight from dozens of helicopter combat assault missions. He later earned his wings as a private pilot owning airplanes he flew primarily to expand his business interests. Bill is a member of the Student Affairs Community Council at the University of North Florida and is a member of the World Affairs Council in Jacksonville, Florida.

Made in the USA
Lexington, KY
29 September 2015